PRUE'S PERFECT GUIDE
TO THE
FISHING PICNIC

By the same author:
Prue's Country Kitchen
Prue's Perfect Guide to the Shoot Lunch

PRUE'S PERFECT GUIDE TO THE FISHING PICNIC

Prue Coats

Illustrated by Ben Hoskyns

WHARNCLIFFE PUBLISHING LIMITED

First published in 1991 by
Wharncliffe Publishing Limited
47 Church Street
Barnsley, South Yorkshire S70 2AS

For up-to-date information on other titles produced
under the Wharncliffe Publishing imprint, please
telephone or write to:

Wharncliffe Publishing Limited
FREEPOST
47 Church Street
Barnsley
South Yorkshire
S70 2BR
Telephone no. (24 hours): (0226) 734555
ISBN 1-871647-053

A CIP catalogue record of this book is available from the British Library

Typeset by Yorkshire Web

Printed in Great Britain at the Alden Press, Oxford

CONTENTS

This book is dedicated to
Archie,
who never gave up

ACKNOWLEDGEMENTS

I should like to thank the following for their invaluable help, advice, and ideas: Ben Hoskyns, for his drawings for the text and cover. Toby Buchan, my editor, and Tony Jackson, who between them hatched the whole plot, and encouraged me. Lucy, for her beady eye, her memory, and all her suggestions. Tania, Constance, Gladys, Jenny, Ann, Camilla, Mrs Vi Davies, Laura, Linda, and all my kind friends who so willingly parted with their precious recipes. My grateful thanks also to the Game Conservancy; to Keith Howman, for allowing me to use extracts from *Prue's Country Kitchen* (World Pheasant Association, 1988); and to the Editors of *Shooting Times & Country Magazine* and of *Countrysport*.

Prue Coats
Dummer, 1991

INTRODUCTION

Archie's love of fishing started as soon as he was big enough to hold a rod. He was lucky enough to live in a twelfth-century castle in Scotland which stood high above the River Coil, named after a Roman general, Coilus. In the early Twenties his father used to take Grogarry Lodge in South Uist where, during one memorable week, they caught a thousand-odd sea trout. Whenever he could escape Nanny's iron grip Archie would join his father or one of his five elder brothers and haul fish out to his heart's content, and he always said this is what started it all off.

My fishing career started far more humbly — and illegally. Just before the war my parents used to take the horses and my pony and a friend's down to Exmoor in the autumn for a month's hunting. My governess, my friend and I stayed in a farmhouse owned by a descendant of R. D. Blackmore, the author of *Lorna Doone*. This was romantic enough, but the two sons of the house were past-masters in the art of 'tickling' trout in the River Barle which ran below the village. My friend and I, having been given a lesson, were anxious to put into practice what we had learnt, so we split up, with me going upstream and him downstream. After several abortive attempts I found a promising rock with a trout lazing away in its shadow. With infinite care I got my hand in the water beneath the fish and began wiggling the water under its belly; then, as it sank almost into my hand, I got my fingers into the gills and with a quick flip hoicked it out. As I was admiring it on the bank I heard heavy footsteps and, to my horror, saw the river bailiff approaching round a bend in the river. Quick as lightning, I stuffed the trout up my knickers. Luckily in those days we wore what were called Regency bloomers, which had elastic round the waist and the legs. The bailiff passed on with a greeting, all unsuspecting, and I heaved a sigh of relief.

My friend, however, would not forgive me for some time, for he thought it most *infra dig* that a mere girl should have succeeded before he did. No fish caught since has ever given me such pleasure.

Food for fishermen is easier to think of than for the shooting party, as in most cases you are only catering for one or two people. Only rarely will you be having a *fête-champêtre,* and even then the maximum number is likely to be two fishermen plus sidekicks and assorted family. Fishing holidays, however, are different altogether, and you will be expected to produce nourishment all round the clock at any time of the night or day, for if the weather is warm the protagonists will want to 'slip down to the river and catch the evening rise' just as you have put supper on the table.

TROUT FISHING — CHALK-STREAMS

CHALK-STREAM LUXURY — MOWN PATHS — FISHING HUT

This, for the fishing wife, is the ultimate in high-living. On most of the chalk-streams where Archie and I were lucky enough to be asked to fish, there was a well-appointed hut with table, wicker armchairs, candle and candlestick. There were also a table and benches outside for those balmy June nights when you could sit there imbibing and watching for rises, listening to the noise of the water tumbling down the weir and, later on, perhaps, the song of a nightingale. Nothing seems to me to embody such a true sense of 'Englishness' as this sort of a scene: the river, clear as gin, meandering through buttercup-strewn water-meadows dotted with cows, swifts and swallows in clouds skimming over the water and, all along the bank, drifts of purple loosestrife, water avens, meadowsweet, comfrey and a host of other almost forgotten wildflowers. The paths you tread to stalk your prey are mown like a lawn, but behind you, lying in wait for the idle cast, are a sea of bulrushes or a line of alder bushes. If, like me, you are a fisher who has more 'off' than 'on' days, such things are positively malign, and on many an occasion when I have been sent off to cast for a particular fish I have been so nervous that I cast badly and frightened it away, or got caught high up in an alder bush and lost Archie's favourite fly. His well-known roar chastened me, and put down any fish in the vicinity. After his operations he could only fish from his shooting seat, hobble along a few yards with me acting as ghillie, and then sit down again. Needless to say there was always a rise out of his reach or too far for him to walk to, so I became his surrogate fisherwoman. He had been a brilliant fisherman before his illness, so for a bungler like me it was a hard act to follow.

I don't think Archie ever grew up, and he was just as enthusiastic in his seventies as he had been in his youth, so we always set off at crack of dawn. Whereas if he was going pigeon shooting ordinary sandwiches were acceptable, he always expected a 'treat' when we went fishing, as well as plenty of 'nibbles' for mid-morning and tea. Two or three courses are quite a good idea for supper as no matter at what time you elect to eat, the 'evening rise' will start and the stuffed egg or whatever will be dropped. You can then come back for your main course, and eat your pudding or cheese just before packing up.

ELEVENSES

Coffee and biscuits are a good idea to break up the morning. Very often you will have had breakfast at crack of dawn before setting off for your day's fishing, so by about midday you will be feeling a bit peckish. I always noticed that if there was nothing much doing on the river, Archie always asked for a titbit.

TANIA'S GINGER SNAPS

Archie did not actually like ginger and quite a lot of people are the same, so it's a good idea to ask any guests beforehand, but for those who do, these are delicious.

---

6 oz/175 g self-raising flour
1 teaspoon bicarbonate of soda
2 oz/50 g butter
4 oz/100 g caster sugar

1 tablespoon golden syrup
1½ tablespoons beaten egg
1 teaspoon ground ginger

Cream together butter, sugar and syrup. Beat in egg and then the dry ingredients to make a firm dough. Turn onto a floured surface, roll into a rope with your hands, cut into little pieces and form into balls. Place on a greased tray, leaving 1-in/3-cm spaces between. Bake in the centre of a pre-heated oven at 350°F/175°C/Gas Mark 4 for 15 minutes.

BROKEN BISCUIT CAKE

One of Archie's favourites — he liked anything to do with 'choccy'. A word of warning, though: anything to do with chocolate is pretty hopeless in hot weather, so keep in a cold-box or insulated bag.

6 oz/175 g plain chocolate	2½ oz/65 g sultanas
2 level tablespoons golden syrup	6 oz/175 g broken digestive biscuits

Melt chocolate and syrup and stir in sultanas and biscuits (broken up in a plastic bag and crushed with a rolling-pin or trodden on!). Turn mixture into a square tin and pack down with a spoon. Leave until set and then cut into squares.

CANDY BARS

Much appreciated by fishermen with a sweet tooth. Most of the ones I know seem to have an over-developed one.

Base	4 oz/100 g margarine
4 oz/100 g margarine	2 oz/50 g caster sugar
2 oz/50 g sugar	1 tablespoon golden syrup
6 oz/175 g plain flour	
	Topping
Filling	6 oz/175 g plain chocolate
1 small tin Nestlé milk	

For the base, cream margarine and sugar until light and creamy, sieve flour and fold in. Press mixture evenly over a greased swiss roll tin and bake in pre-heated oven at 350°F/180°C/Gas Mark 4 for 15 minutes, then cool.

Place all the filling ingredients in a saucepan and melt slowly over a gentle heat until boiling, then continue cooking for 5 minutes stirring constantly. Spread over base and allow to cool.

Melt the chocolate over hot water and pour on top of the filling. Leave until quite cold and cut into squares.

CHEESE BISCUITS

This is really a savoury, but instead of making them into little bundles of straws in a ring, just cut them into squares. They keep best in the freezer and not in a tin. Take them out when you make breakfast and they will be ready to nibble mid-morning.

---

1 oz/25 g flour
1 oz/25 g butter
1½ oz/40 g grated cheese

Cayenne pepper and salt
Yolk of egg, beaten

Rub the butter into the flour (it's hardly worth putting such a small quantity in the Magimix), add the cheese and seasonings and just enough yolk of egg to bind it together. Roll out thinly and cut into squares or rounds and bake in a pre-heated oven at 400°F/200°C/Gas Mark 6 for 5 to 7 minutes.

OTHER NIBBLES

For very hot weather — and for those who are diet-conscious — take along an assortment of *crudités* and a simple dip: sticks of carrot, celery, fennel in a lidded plastic container with a small yogurt pot filled with Taramasalata (smoked cod's roe pâté, see below) or Hummus (chickpea pâté, see below), which you can either make, or if you are feeling idle, buy in most supermarkets; a few mini-pepperami and some kind of hard cheese cut into bite-sized pieces. The dedicated fisherman can dip in almost automatically while he is walking to his next cast, if his hanger-on is kind enough to hand things to him. But beware! Don't, as a hanger-on, on any account let your shadow fall on the water with the sun behind you or you will frighten the fish and be cursed to Hell and high water. How often in my early days did I prance up with the white Tupperware container, metaphorically wagging my tail at being so thoughtful, only to be subjected to one of the Master's roars (readers who knew him will understand what I mean).

HUMMUS

Lucy and I had this, and the next recipe, when we went to Greece and Turkey one year. We managed to prise the recipe out of the chef on the Greek boat we sailed in.

2 cups of cooked garbanzo or chickpeas	*2 - 3 cloves garlic*
1 cup of chickpea water	*1½ teaspoons salt*
1 cup of tahini/sesame seed paste	*Best olive oil*
(obtainable at Sainsbury's)	*1 dessertspoon chopped parsley*
Juice of 1 lemon	

Put the chickpeas, garlic, lemon juice and salt into the Magimix and process. Add enough chickpea liquid and olive oil to make a smooth purée and finally add the parsley. The consistency should be like thick mayonnaise.

TARAMASALATA

This is so easy to make, but doesn't freeze well though it will keep in the fridge for up to a week. Try and get undyed smoked cod's roe if you can.

---

4 oz/100 g smoked cod's roe	*Olive oil*
1 thick slice crustless white bread	*Salt and pepper*
2 teaspoons onion juice	

Soak the bread in water and then squeeze dry (ciabatta bread and Greek olive oil make this really authentic). Peel and cut away any membranes from the cod's roe. Put bread and roe in Magimix and switch on. Pour in enough oil to make a thick, sloppy paste. Add lemon juice to taste, salt and pepper and the onion juice (make this by squeezing chunks of onion or shallot through a garlic press). Chill and eat with bits of pitta or French bread.

If it is a very hot day take a thermos of Spiced Iced Coffee (see below), but if there is one of those nasty biting winds you can have it hot.

SPICED ICED COFFEE

Make 1 cup extra strong coffee with Continental blend instant granules and add 1 teaspoon cloves, a stick of cinnamon and 1 dessertspoon demerara suger and 1 tablespoon brandy (optional). Leave for 5 minutes and then strain and pour over ice. Pour into a thermos and make up the quantity with milk and a dash of cream (optional). If you want to take it hot, just omit the ice.

LUNCHES

Lunch may be the slack time, as if it is very hot the fish will be lying doggo. You can never tell though, so be prepared for a mad dash to that rise he just noticed, and for your beautiful confection to be left untouched. It is best to have a peripatetic menu as he will probably want to eat it on one of those convenient seats dotted at intervals along the bank. These are made from just a plank nailed onto posts in the ground, and in my experience are the most uncomfortable form of seating, so lingering over a gourmet meal won't be the order of the day.

STUFFED LOAF

This is an excellent answer for those who quail at the thought of making raised pie pastry. It can be filled with any kind of minced meat or pâté mixture and, provided it is well wrapped in foil, newspaper and bubble-wrap, will keep hot for quite a long time. If the weather is warm eat it cold.

---

1 small white loaf	*1 raw egg, well beaten*
8 oz/225 g minced veal, pork or turkey	*2 anchovies, finely chopped (optional)*
2 tablespoons Country Herb stuffing	*6 ripe black olives, stoned (optional)*
1 clove garlic, peeled and chopped	*Salt and ground black pepper*
2 shallots, finely chopped	*Oil or butter*
2 hard-boiled eggs	

Serves 2-4

Mix the stuffing with boiling water, cover and leave for 10 minutes. Cut one end off the loaf and pull out the middle. Mix together all the ingredients except the hard-boiled eggs and fill the cavity, then push the two eggs down the middle. Press in well, stick the end on and tie with string. Brush the outside with oil or melted butter and enclose in foil. Cook in a pre-heated oven at 375°F/190°C/Gas Mark 5 for 1 hour. Eat hot or cold cut in thickish slices with a sharp knife.

OMELETTES IN PITTA BREAD

Make 2-egg omelettes, lay a slice of ham over one half, fold over and place in pitta breads previously heated under the grill for 1 minute and then slit down one side to make a pocket.

ITALIAN SNACK

Try and find an Italian ciabatta loaf, which some supermarkets have (whenever I can I stock up with these delectable loaves), or failing that use a French baguette.

---

1 ciabatta or French loaf	*2 tablespoons capers, drained*
4 tablespoons best olive oil	*1 teaspoon parsley, chopped*
4 tablespoons softened butter	*Thin slices Provolone cheese*
1 clove garlic	*Salt and pepper*
1 tin anchovies, drained	

Serves 2

Cut loaf in half lengthwise. Place butter, oil and anchovies in Magimix. Squeeze garlic through press and blend all together. Spread on the bread. Sprinkle on capers and lay on top a thick layer of thinly sliced cheese. Eat with pepperoni and tomatoes.

AVOCADO BAPS

Heat 2 baps in oven until crisp, cut a round out of the top and then pull out all the crumby inside. Peel and stone a ripe avocado and mash together with lemon juice, a hard-boiled egg, and a scrunched-up crisply fried rasher of bacon, salt, pepper, and olive oil. Put a layer of shredded lettuce in the bottom of the bap and then fill with the mixture and replace the 'hat'.

Variation: You can use hazelnut oil and roasted chopped hazelnuts instead of the olive oil and bacon.

For 'afters' in hot weather, have some kind of fruit such as grapes or cherries that can be eaten 'at a stroke' (how many times have I nursed an apple or pear with one bite out of it while Archie went after a fish he had just noticed?). On a cold day, take a KitKat or other favourite chocolate snack/biscuit.

Finally, take something cooling to drink, beer if he is a beer-drinker. Archie wasn't, so I had to come up with a variety of home-made fruity drinks.

LEMON/ELDERFLOWER CORDIAL (to keep)

This is a delectable summer drink, but you do have to take a bit of trouble with it. It will keep for about 3 months in a cool dark cupboard and, once opened, in the fridge for up to 3 weeks.

1 pint/575 ml lemon juice	*1½ pints/850 ml water*
Grated lemon rind	*¼ oz/5 g citric acid*

Wash the lemons and squeeze out the juice, grate the rind of half of them. Add rind to the sugar and water, heat and stir until sugar is dissolved. If flavouring with elderflower add 2-3 heads of elderflower at this point, leave to infuse for 10 minutes, then strain. Add the lemon juice and citric acid to the syrup, stir well then pour into clean, sterilized bottles and sterilize.

Wash bottles — screw-top ones are best. Boil screw-tops and bottles for ten minutes in water, then drain. Pour in cordial to within 2 in/5 cm of the top and seal. Put into a deep pan such as a preserving pan on a wodge of newspaper and fill with cold water nearly to the top of the bottles, which should all be the same height. Raise to simmering point and maintain for 20 minutes. Remove, and as the bottles cool tighten the caps. Dilute to taste.

TROUT FISHING — THE BANKSIDE BANQUET

This is a laid-back kind of piscatorial *fête-champêtre* for when several of a like mind are gathered together by a chalk-stream to unwind after the stresses and strains of a week in the City (or wherever). The ones I best remember included the whole family of our host and hostess, plus ourselves and Lucy. I hate to say it, but all was not always as above-board as it should have been — Lucy, aided and abetted by the son of the house, once caught a whopper by dangling a cigarette butt over the weir. Archie himself was not above a little skulduggery (though we tried to keep this from our kind host), and he was always in the thick of it, egging on the 'unconventional' participants, and dispensing useful advice in what he thought of as a whisper, but which could be heard for miles. Luckily for us, though perhaps not for the owner, the then river-keeper was somewhat venal and could be counted on to turn a blind eye by the liberal application of whisky, to which he was more than somewhat addicted. Don't get me wrong, 99 per cent of the time we were the soul of rectitude and the most law-abiding of citizens, but a combination of wine, the onset of dusk, and Archie plus the younger and more adventurous of the party, could lead us to give way to these baser instincts. I'm afraid Archie never grew up — which is what endeared him to the young. Anyway, it was a long time ago, and after his operations the crutches inhibited much hanky-panky of this sort.

The food for this kind of a banquet should not be strictly divided into courses, but should rather be a kind of smorgasbord so that guests can help themselves at will. Don't forget to take torches and, if it's wet or cold, candles for the hut. It is surprising how chilly and damp it can be on even the most dulcet summer evening once the mist comes down on the river.

CHECK LIST
Plates, tumblers, cutlery
Salt, pepper, sugar
Screw-top jars of salad dressing/mayonnaise
Corkscrew/bottle-opener
Sharp knife
Beer/soft drinks/water/whisky/gin/wine
Cold-box with ice and freezer packs for beer and wine
Insulated bag for beer and wine
Roll of kitchen paper instead of napkins
Anti-midge/mosquito cream/spray
Dog food plus bowls
Rug for those who want to sit on the ground

SUMMER SOUPS

ICED CHICKEN AND LEMON SOUP (AVGOLEMOND)

This Greek soup is usually eaten hot, but it is most refreshing chilled.

1½ pints/850ml concentrated chicken stock　　　*Juice of 2 lemons*
1 glass sherry　　　*Salt and pepper*
4 eggs

Serves 4-6

Heat the stock, which should be really well-flavoured, add the sherry and simmer for 20 minutes. Beat the eggs and lemon juice together until frothy and then gradually whisk in a ladleful of the hot soup. Pour this mixture into the soup and place over a low heat. Go on beating until it begins to thicken *but on no account let it boil.* Season, cool, and refrigerate. Pour into a well-chilled thermos. A suspicion of sugar improves it, I think.

COLD BUTTERMILK SOUP WITH PRAWNS

This sounds an extraordinary combination, but it is quite delicious and very quick and easy to make. Buttermilk is now obtainable at most big supermarkets and health food shops.

1 pint/575ml buttermilk	*or 1 teaspoon dried dill*
4 oz/100 g peeled prawns	*1 dessertspoon made American mustard*
1/4 medium cucumber, peeled	*1/2 teaspoon salt*
1 dessertspoon fresh dill, chopped,	*1 teaspoon sugar*

Serves 2-4

Chop the prawns and cucumber in the Magimix with a few short sharp bursts, then add the rest of the ingredients and mix for a few seconds. Chill well and put into an iced thermos.

CHILLED CRANBERRY BORTSCH

This is a great way to use up those cranberries you have been harbouring in your freezer since Christmas. If you haven't got fresh or frozen berries use cranberry sauce, but if you do, omit the sugar.

4 oz/100 g fresh or frozen cranberries	*1 tablespoon sugar*
or 1 tablespoon sauce	*1 pint/575 ml beef or chicken stock, fresh*
1 large onion, chopped	*or tinned*
4 oz/100 g chopped white cabbage	*1/2 pint/275 ml water*
4 oz/100 g tinned/bottled beets in sweet	*1/4 pint/150 ml sour cream*
vinegar, cut in julienne strips	*2 hard-boiled eggs, finely chopped*
1/4 pint/150 ml beet juice from tin or jar	*Salt and pepper*

Serves 4-6

Stew cranberries in 1/2 pint/275 ml water for 10 minutes and then add onion and cabbage and cook until soft. Blend until smooth in the Magimix and add the stock and then the beet juice. Pour into a bowl, tip in the beets, season and chill. Add chopped eggs and sour cream and pour into a cold thermos. If you haven't got any sour cream, mix 1 teaspoon lemon juice in fresh cream and allow to stand for a quarter of an hour. This soup is equally good hot.

MAIN COURSES

I have not mentioned barbecues as on the beats where we fished the house-rules definitely stated 'no fires', but I suppose the 'throw-away' picnic barbecue now widely available would hardly count. These are not very large so would really only be practical for 2-4 people. I will give some recipes in a separate section later on (see p.91-5) which could be adapted for the chalk-stream supper.

QUICK JAMBON PERSILLÉ

One of the prettiest summer dishes. Most effective made in a white china dish or bowl, but probably more practical to make it in a lidded plastic container for this kind of picnic.

---

1 lb/450 g lean cooked ham cut into chunks
2 tins chicken consommé or
2 cartons fresh chicken stock, obtainable
from large supermarkets
2 shallots, finely chopped
¼ pint/150 ml dry white wine

2 sprigs fresh tarragon
1 bouquet garni
2 packets gelatine
1 tablespoon tarragon vinegar
4 heaped tablespoons finely chopped parsley
Salt and pepper

Serves 2-4

24

Simmer the stock, shallots, bouquet garni and white wine for 20 minutes, then strain. Melt the gelatine in a little of the stock and add it and the tarragon vinegar to the strained liquid. Put the ham into the dish and pour over half the stock and refrigerate until it just begins to set, then mix in the chopped parsley and pour over the rest of the stock. The classical way of making this Burgundian dish takes hours as you cook the ham first with pig's trotters and have to go through all the business of clarifying with egg whites. This is much easier, and just as nice.

ALSATIAN PORK TERRINE

This unusual terrine comes from Strasbourg and was given to me by a friend who lives in a vast château. With great cunning she managed to prise the recipe from her cook.

1 lb/450 g pork	1 carrot, finely chopped
1 lb/450 g veal	2 cloves peeled garlic, finely chopped
1 lb/450 g pork sausagemeat	1 sprig each thyme and parsley
¼ pint/150 ml olive oil	2 bay leaves
½ pint/275 ml dry white wine	Grated nutmeg
2 shallots, finely chopped	Salt and pepper
1 onion, finely chopped	Bacon rashers for lining terrine

Serves 8-10

Cut the pork and veal into ¼-inch/1-cm thin slices and then into 2-inch/5-cm squares. Marinate for 24 hours in the oil, wine, vegetables, and seasonings. Line a terrine with bacon, strain off the marinade and put alternate layers of the meat and sausagement in the terrine. Pour the strained marinade in to come level with the top layer of meat. Cover with more bacon. Cover tightly with foil and then the lid. Cook in a pre-heated oven at 300°F/150°C/Gas Mark 2 for 3 hours. Place a weight on top and refrigerate for 2 or 3 days, to let the flavours develop.

SALMON TART

This French recipe is equally good hot or cold. It will keep warm for several hours if wrapped in foil, then newspaper, and finally bubble-wrap, or, better still, a polystyrene wine case. In order to fit the tart into the case you will have to hack out the bottle divisions with a Stanley knife, but once you've done it you can re-use it on other occasions.

1 lb/450 g salmon	Salt and pepper
1 onion, 1 carrot, 1 leek, 1 stick celery, all finely chopped	Shortcrust Pastry
1 bouquet garni	10 oz/300 g plain flour
Butter	8 oz/225 g butter
3 egg yolks	4 egg yolks
¼ pint/150 ml double cream	Good pinch salt

Serves 4-6

Make shortcrust pastry and chill for 2 hours. Butter some foil generously, lay on the salmon and sprinkle with the vegetables and bouquet garni and seal well, but leave space for the steam to circulate. Put in a pre-heated oven at 300°F/150°C/ Gas Mark 2 for 1 hour. Drain the juice into a bowl, skin the salmon, take out the bones, and put in the Magimix. Add egg yolks and cream and blend until smooth. Line a flan dish with half the pastry, fill with the salmon mixture, roll out the rest of the pastry and cover, sealing all round the edges. Brush with egg yolk beaten with milk and cook in a pre-heated oven at 400°F/200°C/Gas Mark 6 for 10 minutes, then lower the heat to 350°F/175°C/Gas Mark 4 for a further 25 to 30 minutes. Serve hot or cold.

ROULADE OF STUFFED VEAL

This quickly made 'sausage' is an unusual picnic dish. You may not be able to get pig's caul to wrap it in, though any good pork butcher should have one. Buttered foil is the next best thing.

2 large escalopes of veal	2 oz/50 g stoned green olives, finely chopped
2 slices ham	
4 eggs	1 dessertspoon parsley, finely chopped
4 oz/100 g butter	Nutmeg
4 oz/100 g pork sausagemeat	Salt and pepper
3 cocktail gherkins, finely chopped	1 pig's caul, or foil

Serves 2-4

Get your butcher to cut you 2 large veal escalopes, but leave them joined at one end. Ask him to flatten them. Lay the ham on this large 'escalope'. Break the eggs into a saucepan and make rather undercooked, smooth and, as the French would say, 'unctuous' scrambled eggs. Take off the stove and add half the butter cut into small pieces and spread over the ham. Fry the sausagemeat in the rest of the butter and lay on top of the scrambled eggs. Sprinkle with parsley, chopped gherkins, olives, salt, pepper and nutmeg. Roll up into a sausage and encase in the caul, if you've managed to get one. Cook in butter in a pre-heated oven at 400°F/200°C/Gas Mark 6 for 25 to 30 minutes. Failing the caul, wrap in well-buttered foil and cook as above. Allow to get cold and serve in slices.

THE GOODWIFE'S PIGEON CREAM

This is particularly delicious and has the added advantage that the first stage is a recipe on its own, so if the weather turns cold you can simply put it in a wide-mouthed thermos and eat it hot.

Stage 1

5 pigeons	Green Label Mango Chutney
1 lb/450 g onions, roughly chopped	1 chicken stock cube
2 oz/50 g butter	Salt and pepper
4 dessertspoons Major Grey or	

Serves 4-6

Remove the breasts from the pigeons with a sharp knife. Brown the onions in half the butter and then remove to a casserole. Lightly sauté the pigeons' breasts in the rest of the butter until the juices are sealed in, about 1 minute on each side. Lay on top of the onions, crumble the stock cube over them, season and spread with the chutney. Place in a pre-heated oven at 290°F/140°C/Gas Mark 2 for 2 hours or until tender. Meanwhile place the pigeon carcasses in a pan, add a chopped carrot, onion, stalk of celery, bayleaf, teaspoon of mixed herbs and cover with water. Simmer gently while the casserole is cooking.

---

10 pigeon cooked breasts, roughly cut up
1 oz/25 g ham
2oz/50g or 1 oz/25 g butter
2 oz/50 g flour
1 pint/575 ml casserole juice
1½ packets gelatine dissolved in 2
tablespoons stock

½ pint/275 ml double cream whipped to
soft peaks
1 dessertspoon chopped chives
1 dessertspoon chopped parsley
½ teaspoon curry powder
Salt and pepper to taste

Serves 6-8

Process the pigeon breasts and ham roughly in the Magimix. Pour the casserole juice into a jug and make up quantity to 1 pint/575 ml. Dissolve the gelatine in the stock. Melt the butter in a pan, add the flour and cook for a few seconds, then slowly add the juice, stirring constantly until it thickens. Add to the pigeon and ham, together with the chopped herbs, curry powder and gelatine, process for a few short bursts, and season. When quite cool but before it has set, fold in the whipped cream. Transfer to a soufflé dish, or for your river picnic to a plastic container. If you use this for a dinner party at home, spoon into a ring mould and turn out at the last minute. Freezes well.

SALADS

Whatever salads you elect to have do make sure you tear or cut them up small enough to eat with a fork. There is nothing worse than trying to wrestle with a tough piece of lettuce on a wobbly paper plate in the gloaming.

AUBERGINE SALAD

I once had this unusual salad in America and have been trying to work out ever since how it was made. This seems to be the right answer; it makes a good accompaniment to a plain pork terrine or cold chicken.

---

1 lb/450 g aubergine, peeled and diced
4 spring onions cut into thin rings
1 oz/25 g finely chopped green pepper
(optional)
8 oz/225 g tomatoes, peeled and de-seeded
1 clove garlic, peeled and finely chopped
1 teaspoon chopped parsley
Sesame seeds (optional)

Dressing
1 teaspoon white wine vinegar
1 dessertspoon lemon juice
1/4 pint/150 ml olive or sesame oil
1 teaspoon salt
1 teaspoon sugar
Ground black pepper

Cook the diced aubergine in boiling salted water for 8–10 minutes. It should be firm and just tender. Drain, cool and mix with the other ingredients. Make the dressing and when chilled add and mix well. Pack in a lidded plastic container and sprinkle with sesame seeds (optional).

FRENCH BEAN SALAD

You can also make this with whole, *small* runner beans. Your gardener, be he husband or the so-many-hours-a-week kind, will believe you are committing infanticide, but I think it's the only way to eat runner beans, and prevents that awful glut of hard-carapaced monsters with fully formed beans inside which will inundate your kitchen otherwise.

1 lb/450 g fine green beans or baby runners	*3 tablespoons best cold-pressed olive oil*
4 rashers streaky bacon grilled until crisp,	*1 dessertspoon wine vinegar*
crumbled up	*1 teaspoon sugar*
2 spring onions, chopped	*Salt and pepper*
2 hard-boiled eggs, chopped	

Top and tail the beans and cook in boiling, salted water for 5 minutes. They should still be *al dente* and bright green. Drain and cool, then add the other ingredients except the bacon and mix well. Put in a lidded plastic container and take the bacon separately and add at the moment of serving.

ASPARAGUS SALAD

This is not so extravagant as it sounds as you can buy 'sprue' or very thin green stalks of asparagus reasonably, and I think these have even more flavour than the fat, forced kind.

1 lb/450 g sprue	*1 dessertspoon chopped parsley*
1 hard-boiled egg, finely chopped	*Lemon mayonnaise with soft cheese*

Trim the ends of the sprue and cook in boiling, salted water for 5 minutes. Drain and lay carefully in a shallow lidded plastic container. Make a lemon mayonnaise with 2 egg yolks, ½ pint/275 ml olive oil, lemon juice, salt, pepper and 2 oz/50 g soft cheese. Add the hard-boiled egg and parsley and take separately in a screw-top jar.

MANGETOUT AND CARROT SALAD

Another of Lucy's finds when she was in America. It can also be made with sugar snap peas.

1 lb/450 g mangetout or sugar snap peas	*1 tablespoon sugar*
1 lb/450 g baby new carrots	*1 tablespoon mint, chopped*
1 tablespoon sunflower oil	*Salt and pepper*
1 dessertspoon wine vinegar	

Top and tail and string the peas if they need it, and top and tail and scrape the carrots. Drop the carrots into boiling salted water for 5 minutes, then add the peas and cook for a further 3 minutes. Drain and cool slightly, then mix in the rest of the ingredients. You can if you wish replace the wine vinegar with tarragon vinegar and the mint with tarragon.

SALADE CAUCHOISE

A delicious potato salad from Normandy, where I first met it many years ago when I was visiting stud farms in the course of my work with a bloodstock agency.

1 lb/450 g potatoes	¼ pint/150 ml sour cream
8 oz/225 g centre and inner leaves of celery cut into julienne strips	1 tablespoon wine vinegar Juice of ½ a lemon
4 oz/100 g ham cut in julienne strips	Salt and pepper
7 fl oz/200 ml double cream	

Large new, or waxy old, potatoes are best. Cook them in their skins, cool slightly and peel, then cut into 1½-inch x ¼-inch/4-cm x 1-cm batons. Make a dressing by whipping the double cream until it is just beginning to thicken. Add the sour cream, vinegar, lemon juice and seasonings, pour it over the rest of the ingredients and mix well, taking care not to break up the potatoes.

SWEDISH POTATO SALAD

This colourful salad recipe was given to me by my Swedish sister-in-law.

2 lbs/900 g peeled and sliced cooked potatoes	1 tablespoon capers
2 tablespoons each chopped parsley, chervil and tarragon	1 tablespoon chopped chives 1 tablespoon wine vinegar
3 tablespoons finely chopped pickled beetroot	6 tablespoons best olive oil Salt and pepper
	1 tablespoon finely shredded leek

Put the potatoes, which should still be warm, into bowl, sprinkle over the beetroot, capers and herbs and pour on the oil, vinegar and seasoning and mix well. Garnish with finely shredded leek.

PUDDINGS AND DRINKS

On the whole I would eschew 'afters' because when you come to eat them it is probably too dark to see, or if it has been a difficult or fishless day your loved ones will have their minds set on a fish or on 'getting their limit'. However much they may say they love the scenery, and so forth, the hunting instinct generally prevails, so that just as you have dished out some scrummy pudding everyone will have vanished and you will be left to clear up the debris. Fruit or cheese are easier to deal with. I will, however, give a few recipes for the Bankside Banquet puddings, since if there are young around they are always ready to scoff anything that is going.

Drinks are another matter, though — a bottle of whisky so that the oldies can have a nip to restore their flagging spirits, plenty of home-made lemonade (see p.19), wine, the ingredients for kir and/or spritzer, and perhaps some sparkling Normandy cider. Not too much though, or you may repeat the situation Archie found himself in just after the war. He was fishing a trout river in Normandy on a very hot day in the summer and had forgotten to take anything to drink, so he trudged up to a farmhouse and asked the farmer if he could have a drink of water. '*Eau*, no!' (with apologies to a certain advertisement), said the farmer, 'I will get you something better'. He plonked Archie down in the farm kitchen and disappeared into the cellar, and presently came up bearing a large leather-covered bottle from which he poured some golden nectar into glasses. Archie swigged it down and was then given another, and then another... They discussed all manner of things, the war, politics, and fishing. Finally Archie said he must be going, but when he tried to get out of the chair his legs just wouldn't work, though he said his brain was as clear as a bell. The farmer roared with laughter and finally came clean. He said it was a ten-year-old vintage cider and he realised that Archie did not know how potent it was but he had wanted to see how much the Englishman could drink. After an hour or two Archie recovered enough to leave, but he never said whether he caught any more trout.

PUDDINGS

Here are two nice gooey cakes that can be taken along in their baking tins.

GREEK LEMON CAKE

8 oz/225 g softened butter	1 teaspoon baking powder
12 oz/350 g caster sugar	1 tablespoon lemon peel
4 eggs	½ pint/275 ml plain yogurt
10 oz/300 g plain flour	4 oz/100 g chopped nuts
1 teaspoon bicarbonate of soda	¼ pint/150 ml lemon juice

Serves 6-8

Sift together the flour, bicarbonate of soda and baking powder. Cream the butter and 8 oz/225 g of the sugar together in the Magimix until light and fluffy. Add lemon peel and, alternately, the flour mixture and yogurt. Finally, fold in the chopped nuts. Spoon into a 9-in/22-cm loaf tin and bake in a pre-heated oven at 350°F/175°C/Gas Mark 4. Dissolve the remaining sugar in the lemon juice in a saucepan over a low heat and pour whilst still hot over the cake. Leave to cool and serve out of the tin.

MEDITERRANEAN ORANGE CAKE

4 oz/100 g softened butter	2 tablespoons grated orange peel
8 oz/225 g caster sugar	4 oz/100g chopped nuts
3 eggs	
8 oz/225 g wholemeal flour	Topping
1 teaspoon baking powder	
1 teaspoon bicarbonate of soda	2 oz/50 g caster sugar
¼ teaspoon ground cardamom	3 fl oz/80 ml Cointreau
7 fl oz/200 ml buttermilk	½ pint/275 ml orange juice

Serves 10-12

Make this cake at least one if not two days ahead of time so that it can get really gooey. Sift together the flour, baking powder, bicarbonate of soda and cardamom. Cream together the butter and sugar in the Magimix and then beat in the eggs one by one. Blend in the flour mixture and buttermilk alternately and, finally, fold in the nuts and orange peel. Butter and flour a 9-inch/22-cm loaf tin and bake in a pre-heated oven at 350°F/175°C/Gas Mark 4 for 55 minutes. Combine all the topping ingredients and make sure that the sugar has dissolved completely. Whilst it is still hot, pierce the top of the cake with a skewer and pour the liquid slowly all over it so that it all seeps in. Serve from the baking tin.

KATAIFI

This is a delicious Middle Eastern sweet which can be made with Shredded Wheat, since you are most unlikely to be able to get the kataifi pastry in this country.

12 Shredded Wheats
1¼ pints/725 ml milk
2 tablespoons caster sugar
8 oz/225 g butter, melted
2 oz/50 g shelled pistachio nuts or pine kernels, chopped
8 oz/225 g walnut pieces

Syrup
2 oz/50 g caster sugar
3 fl oz/80 ml water
1 teaspoon lemon juice
¼ pint/150 ml honey

Serves 6-8

Split the Shredded Wheats in half and dip in milk. Lay 12 halves in a 10-inch/25-cm square baking tray. Sprinkle with 2 tablespoons sugar, pour on half the melted butter and top with the chopped nuts. Cover with the other 12 halves. Pour on the rest of the melted butter, let it soak in and then press everything down firmly. Bake in a pre-heated oven at 350°F/175°C/Gas Mark 4 for 30 minutes until nicely browned. Make a syrup with the sugar, water, honey and lemon juice and pour over the biscuits whilst still hot. Cover and cool, then cut into 2-inch/5-cm squares. Very sticky, so remember to take kitchen paper which can be dipped in the river and used to wipe hands. Pukka fishermen would not like to find goo all over their precious rod-handles!

DRINKS

If the weather is hot, don't forget to take your cold-box and some ice, though bottles in a string bag or sack sunk in the river and securely anchored to a bush keep wonderfully cool. Apart from nice refreshing and thirst-quenching cordials or the like, it is a good idea to take a thermos of coffee (or boiling water and a jar of instant granules or tea bags) to give you the energy to collect up all the clobber and hit the road for home, especially if you have far to drive. No prizes for guessing who will be the chauffeur/se. Your fisherman will be exhausted by all the effort he has put into his hunter-gatherer activities and will have restored his energy in the time-honoured way while you have limited yourself to one measly glass of wine.

ELDERFLOWER WINE

This was our favourite home-made wine, and is just the sort of thing to drink on the river bank on a hot summer's evening with the heady smell of the elderflowers wafting across the river. If you make it one year and have enough strength of mind to keep it for twelve months you will find that in June, when the flowers are at their peak, the wine will become quite *pétillant* and bubbly. Not being a scientific sort of wine-maker I was never able to regulate the dryness or otherwise, so that mine usually turned out to be more of a dessert wine. Our great friend Ralph, now alas no longer with us, once came to stay in the days when he was Managing Director of a very well-known wine firm. We played a trick on him and served a particularly good vintage with a napkin wrapped round the bottle and asked him to give us his opinion. He went through all the usual rigmarole of sniffing, snuffing, rolling round the palate, and so on. He finally said that he thought it was a Frontignan dessert wine. Luckily he had a wonderful sense of humour and thoroughly enjoyed the joke, so much so, in fact, that he begged a bottle so that he could try it out in his Directors' lunch room. They were completely taken in, but being less generous than him took it in rather bad part.

You will have to bear with me as this recipe is a bit long-winded, but it is aimed at those who would like to make a few bottles but don't know how to begin. They can then decide if they want to branch out into more complicated equipment (Boots is the best place to get it all).

Equipment
1 large china wash-basin or plastic pail
1-gallon glass fermentation jar
1 fermentation lock
1 length of plastic tubing
1 bottle Campden sterilizing tablets
(sulphur dioxide)
1 large cork to fit fermentation jar with
hole to take lock
1 large cork to fit fermentation jar to seal
6 wine bottles, carefully washed, dried and
sterilized
6 wine-bottle corks

1 packet plastic bottle-tops
1 tonic water or soda water bottle with cap
2 plastic funnels, 1 large and 1 small

Ingredients for the Wine

1 pint/575 ml creamy white elderflower
florets, well pressed down
2 lemons
2 rounded teaspoons Boots wine yeast
compound
3 lbs/1.4 kg sugar
1 gallon/4.5 litres boiling water

Wash and sterilize all the equipment according to the instructions on the bottle of Campden tablets. 6 hours before you start prepare the wine yeast compound by mixing 2 rounded teaspoons in ¼ pint/150 ml tepid water and then pouring it into the tonic/soda water bottle. Screw cap on tightly and shake well, then loosen and leave at room temperature for 6 hours. Pick the elderflowers on a dry, sunny day, then snip off the florets with a pair of scissors and press into a pint measure, then tip into a sterilized china bowl or plastic bucket. Peel the lemons very thinly, removing all pith, and add to the florets, together with the sugar. Pour on the boiling water and stir well to dissolve the sugar. Leave until it has reached blood heat or until it feels tepid on the back of the hand, then pour in the yeast compound. Cover with a clean tea-towel and leave for 3 days at room temperature, stirring twice daily.

Strain the wine and pour into the jar. Insert the cork and fit the fermentation lock into the hole. Take the top off and half-fill the lock with water. Replace top. Leave in the kitchen or similar at room temperature until the lock has stopped making rude noises, about 6 weeks. Don't do what a friend of mine — a fanatic wine-maker who lived in a London flat — did. He used to keep his fermentation jars in his wife's airing cupboard. One night there was a terrific explosion, which at first he thought was an IRA bomb (he was ex-Army). It was just too hot in the cupboard and all the six jars had exploded.

Take out the air lock. Place the bucket at a lower level than the jar. Insert the tubing into the jar with one end in the bucket. Contort yourself so that you can suck the bucket end of the tube and get the juice flowing into the bucket. Keep the tube end in the jar always just above the level of the yeast sediment. Continue until you have all the juice except the sediment in the bucket. Wash and sterilize the jar well and pour back the wine. Cork tightly and leave in a cool dark place until it is crystal clear, at the end of which time pour into clean, sterilized bottles, leaving any sediment at the bottom of the jar. Soak the corks in boiling water and force into the bottles using a wooden mallet and small wooden wedge to drive them in; an ordinary hammer will do, but don't smash the bottles. Put on the plastic 'hats' and leave to mature for as long as possible.

HOME-MADE GINGER BEER

1 lemon	1 oz/25 g bruised dried ginger pieces
½ oz/15 g cream of tartar	1 tablespoon brewer's yeast
1 lb/450 g white sugar	1½ gallons/7 litres water

Pare the lemon thinly then squeeze out the juice and remove any pips. Put the peel, juice, ginger, cream of tartar, sugar and yeast into a large sterilized bowl or plastic bucket and pour on the boiling water. Cover with a clean tea-towel and leave in a warm place for 12 hours. Skim off the yeast and pour into another clean sterilized container. Without disturbing the sediment pour into sterilized bottles and screw down corks. Keep in a cool dark place.

SOUTH SEAS SPIKED TEA

Lucy picked up this recipe on her honeymoon in Bali. It contains a ferocious amount of rum. I have given the quantity in full, but think perhaps half would be enough.

Juice of 1 lemon	½ pint/275 ml Lamb's Navy Rum
4 oz/100 g caster sugar	Slices of lemon
2 pints/1 litre strong tea	

Make the tea, strain into a jug and add the sugar, lemon juice and rum. Stir well until sugar is completely dissolved, Cool, and when chilled pour into an iced thermos. Take a small plastic bag with lemon slices to float in each tumbler. Can also be drunk hot, in cold weather.

QUINCE BRANDY

I make no apology for including this liqueur as I think it is one of the most delicate and delicious home-made ones that I know. I realize that very few people have a quince tree, but it is likely that someone in your neighbourhood has, so you can beg a couple of the exquisite, golden pear-shaped fruits. In Spain they are quite common and the Spaniards make a kind of quince paste which they eat with cheese, and in many of the keepers' houses in the rural 'outback' you will see the fruit hanging up in the kitchen to ripen alongside ears of maize and all kinds of peppers. Their scent is quite overpowering. A quince tree — *Cydonia oblonga* 'Lusitanica' — was almost one of the first things I planted when we came here and every year it seems to produce a mass of fruit — perhaps it knows I love it! Those of you with gardens, even in towns, may have a *Chaenomeles japonica* or Japanese Quince growing up your house. You can use these fruits, but they are not so aromatic and you would have to use 4 instead of 2.

---

2 large quinces
Caster sugar
¼ teaspoon each ginger and mace

1 stick cinnamon
Brandy

Rub the down off the quinces, rinse under the tap, cut into suitable pieces (don't peel or core), and grate in the Magimix. Put the grated quince in the bottom of a 2-pint/1-litre bottling jar or an empty catering-size Hellman's mayonnaise jar, well washed-out and sterilized. Fill with sugar to one-third of the way up the jar, add the spices and fill up with brandy. Keep for as long as possible before straining into clean, sterilized bottles, and try not to drink it too soon — the longer it is kept the better. If you become as hooked as I am you will have to double or even treble the quantity. On a very hot evening it is nice *frappé*, that is, poured over ice.

TROUT FISHING — STILLWATER LAKES

Archie and I fished a number of stillwater lakes and reservoirs. My most cherished memories are of fishing the Elan Valley reservoirs, and Claerwen in particular. We first went there in its heyday just after it had been opened by Her Majesty the Queen. Fisherfolk were tougher in those days. The lake is eight miles long and the track — you couldn't call it a road — only went half-way up one side. Archie's theory was that the further you walked, the less the likelihood that your chosen spot would have been over-fished, so we used to trudge round to a point opposite where we had left the car. All the fishing stuff had to go with us, as well as a small camping stove fuelled by solid meths blocks, a small frying-pan, butter, salt, pepper, and a plastic bag of coarse oatmeal. We often used to catch our limit, and on one occasion I actually caught the heaviest fish of the day. It was wonderful — the haunting cry of the curlew, the harsh croak of a pair of ravens, the skylarks, and a feeling of emptiness and peace. You would fish round little points and, if you were lucky, be rewarded with the scream of the reel and finally the thrill when you got your first look at the golden-brown, spotted fish on the end of your line. It was very boggy, with lots of cottongrass, and in your excitement you probably fell in, but it didn't matter. I soon learned to fillet a fish, for Archie hated bones. We used to light our little stove, melt the butter (if it hadn't already done so and seeped into all the fly-boxes) and fry our trout with oatmeal. Washed down with hot, sweet tea and a slug of whisky, I don't think anything has ever tasted so good.

The Elan Valley reservoirs are owned by Birmingham City Corporation. On one never-to-be-forgotten occasion Archie spied a man walking over the crest of the hill with a rod, bag, gun, cartridge-bag and dog. Thinking that has was a poacher, Archie walked up to him and asked him what the Hell he thought he was doing with a gun and a rod on BCC land. He roared with laughter; it transpired that he was the Secretary and had been shooting grouse and decided to catch the 'evening rise'.

If, like us, you were in a B&B it was self-catering for lunch and then either a lakeside fry-up or fish and chips in the local 'caff' for supper, as we didn't have many pennies in those days. Luckily there was always a wealth of wonderful Welsh bread, potato scones and the like, so, given plenty of ham, Welsh butter, cheese, onion and pickle, a haversack lunch was ready in no time. Sometimes I could not face my cooked breakfast, so that would be surreptitiously sandwiched between bits of toast. Apples and chocolate and some kind of sticky cake or bun assuaged Archie's sweet tooth, and our thermos of tea with a flask of whisky completed the day's menu. There wasn't such a variety of food available in those days, but what there was was good, and the ham very often home-cooked. I don't think, even nowadays, I could suggest anything much better.

My worst disaster happened when Archie suddenly decided, on the spur of the moment, to go and fish the Teifi Pools Cardigan. He had only the name of the keeper, and said we would probably be able to find somewhere to stay. When we arrived, the only pub was full of commercial travellers and there was nowhere else to stay, so we were left with Hobson's choice and had to sleep in our Thames van. I was three months pregnant with Lucy, and Archie, Simba (our large yellow labrador) and I slept in the back of the van, or rather they did, as they stretched out diagonally on three-quarters of the floor space, leaving

me (and Lucy) the other corner! When not fishing Archie shot duck and snipe all over the wonderful local marsh. Just before he died, Archie and I went to supper with some friends, where the other guests proved to be the owner of the marsh which Archie had, all unwittingly, poached with their keeper! They had finally caught the keeper out by returning a day early from London and finding tents all over their lawn — Frank had been letting it out to campers for years, in addition to his nefarious duck and snipe activities. They couldn't sack him, for he had been with the family for years, so he was just pensioned off with a caution.

BOAT AND BANK

Haversack rations are best for both these venues, as if you are to be a 'banker' you will have to walk to your pitch, and in a boat you won't want anything too bulky. Most commercial fisheries prohibit fires, so barbecues in summer are out of the question unless you are the guest of a private fishery when, of course, you can have a Bankside Banquet as described in the previous section. If you are in a boat don't take a basket as it will only get in the way, but you can take one or two large haversacks, game bags or even plastic bags — one for the food and one for the thermoses and booze. Food which is easy to eat is essential, since you or your companion will have to combine casting, retrieving the line, rowing and eating all at one time. That is, if your man is anything like Archie, who would never actually stop fishing for a meal, and had to be fed rather like a baby. Even in warm weather hot soup is nice, as it can be quite chilly out on the water. Pack one lidded plastic container with the sandwiches and one with cakes or sweet things. Fruit can go in another one.

SOUPS

CAULIFLOWER

1 large cauliflower	1 bay leaf
4 oz/100 g onion, peeled and chopped	1/4 pint cream, fromage frais or 1
4 oz/100 g potato, peeled and chopped	dessertspoon grated cheese
1 clove garlic, peeled and chopped	1 teaspoon sugar
2 oz/50 g butter	1 dessertspoon chopped chives
1 1/2 pints/850 ml water	Salt and pepper

Serves 2-4

Cut off all the cauliflower florets and put them in a pan with the butter, onion, garlic and potato. Cook over a low heat with the lid on for 5 to 10 minutes, shaking occasionally. Add enough water to cover, then the bay leaf, sugar and seasonings, and simmer until soft. Remove bay leaf and blend soup in the Magimix until smooth, then add the rest of the water and bring to the boil. Remove from stove, sprinkle in the chives and add cream, fromage frais or cheese. Pour into a heated thermos.

CHESTNUT AND APPLE

TRICK OF THE TRADE. Don't panic, it is quite unnecessary to peel the chestnuts. If you have a local Sainsbury's buy a couple of packs of frozen button sprouts with chestnuts. Remove the sprouts, re-bag them and put back in the freezer. Otherwise use tinned chestnuts, but they don't have quite the flavour.

---

12 oz/350 g peeled chestnuts
4 oz/100 g onion, peeled and chopped
4 oz/100 g apple, peeled and chopped
2 oz/50 g butter
2 pints/1 litre chicken stock (or water and

a stock cube)
¼ pint/150 ml yogurt or cream
1 teaspoon sugar
Salt and pepper

Serves 2-4

Sauté the onion and apple until soft and then add the chestnuts, sugar, salt and pepper. Cover with stock and simmer for 20 minutes, then liquidize. Pour in the rest of the stock and bring to the boil. Add yogurt or cream, stir well and pour into a heated thermos.

PARSNIP AND CIDER

This soup comes into the category of being detrimental to the ozone layer, so is best eaten outside.

---

1 large parsnip, peeled and cut up	a stock cube)
1 onion, peeled and chopped	½ pint/275 ml cider
1 clove of garlic, peeled and crushed	1 dessertspoon chopped parsley
2 tablespoons sunflower oil	Salt and pepper
1 pint/275 ml chicken stock (or water and	

Serves 2-4

Cook the onion and garlic in the oil over a low heat until transparent, add the parsnip and cider and cook, covered, until soft. Blend in Magimix until smooth and then pour in the seasonings and parsley and bring to the boil. Put into a heated thermos. Instead of the cider you can use lemon or orange juice and a touch of curry powder.

CHICKEN BREASTS EN CROÛTE

These are nicest eaten hot or warm, so put them in the oven whilst you are having breakfast, wrap in foil and pack them into a lidded plastic container, where they will retain a certain amount of heat. There is nothing worse than pastry-wrapped food straight out of the fridge, cold, tasteless and soggy.

---

2 skinned chicken breasts	Mild Dijon mustard
¾ pint/425 ml chicken stock	Dried or chopped fresh tarragon
¼ pint/150 ml sherry	4 thin slices Emmental or Gruyère cheese
4 sprigs tarragon	Frozen puff pastry, thawed out
4 thin slices ham	Beaten egg

Serves 4

Heat the stock and sherry until boiling and pull off stove. Put in the chicken breasts and tarragon sprigs, cover tightly and place on a very low heat, if possible on a heat-reducing mat. Poach for 20 minutes then remove, drain, cool and split in half lengthwise. Spread ham with mustard, sprinkle with tarragon and wrap round each chicken breast and then finally wrap round a slice of cheese. Roll the pastry out very thinly and cut into 4-inch/10-cm circles, place a chicken breast on each one, fold over pastry, wet the rim and press together with a fork. Brush with beaten egg and bake in a pre-heated oven at 400°F/200°C/Gas Mark 6 for 20 minutes until puffed and golden.

TYROPOKITA

This delicious Greek dish can be eaten hot or cold. If baked just before you leave and packed in a single layer in a container, then covered in foil, it will stay warm for several hours.

1 packet frozen puff pastry, thawed out	*½ pint/275 ml finely chopped fresh spinach*
1 lb/450 g feta cheese, crumbled	*leaves*
3 tablespoons lemon juice	*2 tablespoons parsley, finely chopped*
3 tablespoons onion, finely chopped	*2 egg yolks*
1 clove garlic, peeled and finely chopped	*2 egg whites*
3 tablespoons mint, finely chopped	*1 pinch cinnamon*
1 teaspoon dried oregano	*Salt and ground black pepper*

Serves 4-6

In a large bowl mix together the cheese, onion, garlic, lemon juice, spinach, herbs, salt, pepper and *egg yolks*. Roll the pastry out very thinly on a floured board and cut into 7-inch/18-cm circles. On each half-circle place several tablespoons of the filling and sprinkle lightly with cinnamon. Brush the edges of the pastry with lightly beaten egg whites and fold over. Press together and crimp edges with a fork. Brush tops with remaining egg white and bake in a pre-heated oven at 375°F/190°C/Gas Mark 5 for 25 minutes.

STUFFED EGGS

Stuffed hard-boiled eggs are an excellent appetite blunter and are easy to eat. There are lots of different mixtures you can use that get away from the stereotyped curried egg.
TRICK OF THE TRADE. Whatever ingredient you decide to mix with the egg yolks always use a small proportion of butter, which, when cold, will help to hold it together.

1. *Finely chopped celery, mayonnaise, finely chopped spring onion, Dijon mustard and toasted sesame seeds.*

2. *Mayonnaise, horseradish, smoked trout or mackerel, finely chopped fennel bulb and lemon juice.*

3. *Chopped capers, anchovies, finely chopped parsley and stoned black olives.*

4. *Chopped black olives, feta cheese, olive oil.*

SANDWICHES

The Americans make the best sandwiches I know, imaginative, and with more filling than bread. The other very important thing is to include some kind of crunchy texture to make it more interesting. You can use all kinds of different ingredients — bean sprouts, crisp bacon, nuts, celery, apple, and so on.

1. *Cream cheese with finely chopped spring onion, Danish caviar and very finely chopped beetroot in a hollowed-out wholemeal salad bap.*

2. *Small soft rolls crisped in the oven, a hole cut in the top, the middle pulled out and filled with quail's eggs and lemony home-made mayonnaise.*

3. *Grated carrot, finely shredded cabbage, raisins and Hellman's mayonnaise.*

4. *Finely shredded cooked chicken mixed with mayonnaise, soy sauce, a teaspoon of very finely chopped fresh ginger and fresh coriander leaves.*

SWEET SANDWICH SPREADS

1. *Stewed apricot, chopped nuts and cream cheese.*

2. *Thick-cut marmalade and cream cheese.*

3. *Crisp bacon scrunched up and mixed with thick honey or cream cheese and maple syrup.*

BISCUITS AND CAKES

Of course you can always take bought chocolate biscuit snacks, but home-made ones are much nicer, so here are a couple of recipes to ring the changes with.

BELGIAN BISCUITS

This is a really easy 'no bake' variety which takes no time at all to make and keeps well in a tin.

---

4 oz/100 g margarine or butter
1 tablespoon golden syrup
1 tablespoon sultanas
1 oz/25 g chopped walnuts

4 tablespoons drinking chocolate
8 oz/225 g crushed digestive biscuits
Melted chocolate to cover

Serves 2-4

Melt together the butter and syrup and add the sultanas, nuts and drinking chocolate. Mix well and add the crushed digestive biscuits. Press into a baking tin and leave to set. Pour over melted chocolate and when it is just beginning to harden cut into squares. Not recommended for a very hot day, as it will melt and get sticky.

GINGER BUTTER CAKES

This recipe was given to me by one of our many American friends who used to come over and shoot pigeons with Archie.

8 oz/225 g softened butter	*10 oz/300 g sifted, unbleached flour*
12 oz/350 g sugar	*½ teaspoon ground ginger*
1 egg, beaten	*2 tablespoons crystallized ginger, chopped*

Serves 4-6

Cream together the butter and sugar in the Magimix, add the two kinds of ginger and all but 1 tablespoon of the egg, then blend in the flour, a few tablespoons at a time. Turn the mixture onto a floured surface and knead for a few minutes, place in a well-buttered 8-inch/20-cm cake tin and pat out flat. Brush with the remaining tablespoon of egg and bake in a pre-heated oven at 350°F/175°C/Gas Mark 4 for 45 minutes, or until golden brown. Cool for 30 minutes then turn out of pan and cut into serving pieces. It will harden as it cools. These cakes will keep for a long time in an airtight tin.

TROUT FISHING — INACCESSIBLE LOCHS, STREAMS, BURNS

Many is the time I have toiled up behind Archie to some faraway loch which he had heard of. He always thought that these waters would hold the ultimate 'monster', or perhaps a good bag of little trout, and that because they were so far from the beaten track no one else would have fished them. Alas, too often when we got there we found signs that others had been before us. It wasn't quite so bad with two of us to share the burden, but if you are on your own you don't want to carry too much more than your rod, fishing bag, net, Barbour and wellies. If the weather is Mediterranean down below in the strath or glen don't be misled, it can be utterly different a few hundred feet up and quite often a thick mist may come down suddenly and you will be glad of something hot and sustaining to drink, so I think a thermos is a 'must'. Food should be sustaining but not bulky, and some dried fruit is a good idea as it gives instant energy.

Archie was extremely prone to seasickness, and one of my most vivid memories is of a storm which got up on a loch on the island of Islay, where we had gone to recuperate from the stresses of being Game Fair secretaries at Hackwood Park. This is a very large loch, but nowhere is it more than four feet deep. The wind was getting stronger and stronger. I was rowing, but the boat, caught by the gale, kept slipping past our landing-point. As I yelled to Archie to take the oars I noticed him being sick over the side. Eventually, as we scudded backwards, I managed to steer the boat into an inlet where we had to stay until the storm had died down and we could continue our fishing.

One of my last memories of fishing a Highland loch was a few years ago when we were asked to stay with some cousins at a lodge they had taken. Archie was very crippled by then, and on crutches. The rest of the party were going stalking so Archie's cousin and our other host volunteered to heave the Master into the boat. This had to be the actual procedure, as where the boat was moored there was no bank or landing-stage. Off we set and were motoring up the loch, preparatory to doing a long drift down it, when we saw a small black dot swimming towards us. As it got nearer we made out that it was the very elderly fat black labrador belonging to the other guests. They had gone stalking, and their dog had obviously mistaken us for them. We had to cut the engine in case it got caught up in the propeller and Archie, who was immensely strong in the arms, managed to haul it into the boat. By now we were drifting at a terrific rate, so we tried to re-start the engine. Neither of us being very good mechanics we failed utterly, and were swept with great force to the farther shore, where we had to wait until help came. It was no good my going back to the lodge, because everyone was out. It was bitterly cold, raining and blowing, and we were marooned for several hours. Notwithstanding, Archie made me somehow get him out of the boat, which nearly capsized in the process, he being no lightweight. He then proceeded to fish and to suggest that I do the same, for, as he said, 'we mustn't waste good fishing time'.

Here are some suggestions for a haversack lunch.

LUNCH BOXES

1. Bap filled with 2 grilled lamb cutlets, de-boned, chopped finely and mixed with redcurrant jelly. Sandwich of chopped dates and cream cheese.

2. Chicken breast filled with cream cheese and sweetcorn (see below). Brown bap, hollowed out and filled with brown sugar and banana.

3. Bap generously filled with chopped hard-boiled egg, sardine and mayonnaise. Country Cake (see below).

4. 2 Glamorgan Sausages (see below) each in a long roll or hoagie. Country Snacks (see below).

CHICKEN BREAST FILLED WITH CREAM CHEESE AND SWEETCORN

This is a kind of Maryland Chicken, quite delicious eaten cold, and very sustaining.

1 - 2 skinned chicken breasts	*Southern Fried Chicken coating*
Flour for dredging	*2 tablespoons cream cheese mixed with corn*
1 egg, beaten	*kernels*
Coarse dried breadcrumbs or packet	*Oil for frying/baking*

Serves 1-2

Insert a sharp knife down one side of each chicken breast and make a pocket. Fill them with a mixture of cream cheese and corn kernels and then roll in flour. Coat in egg and breadcrumbs and then sauté in oil in a heavy frying-pan until brown on each side. Transfer to a pre-heated oven at 300°F/150°C/Gas Mark 2 for 30-40 minutes, or until tender. Remove and cool on kitchen paper.

GLAMORGAN SAUSAGES

A relic of the days when meat was a luxury.

3 oz/75 g fresh breadcrumbs	*2 tablespoons milk*
2 oz/50 g Caerphilly or other crumbly	*2 egg yolks*
cheese such as feta	*2 egg whites*
1 small leek or onion, finely chopped	*Flour*
1 dessertspoon parsley, chopped	*Salt and pepper*
¼ teaspoon mustard powder	

Serves 2

Process the cheese in the Magimix. Tip into a bowl and mix with the leek/onion, parsley, breadcrumbs, mustard powder, 2 egg yolks, 1 egg white, salt and pepper. Pour in enough milk to bind, shape into 2 large sausages and coat in the remaining egg white, beaten until frothy. Roll in the flour and fry in oil for 10 minutes or until golden.

COUNTRY CAKE

A wonderful no-cook cake. Highly recommended to all mothers as no trouble to make and very healthy.

---

8 oz/225 g seedless raisins	*8 oz/225 g walnuts*
8 oz/225 g stoned dates	*8 oz/225 g almonds*
8 oz/225 g dried apricots	*4 fl oz/80 ml orange juice*
8 oz/225 g dried apples	

Serves 8-10

Blend everything in Magimix until finely ground, then add orange juice. Press firmly into an 8-inch/20-cm × 4½-inch/11-cm well-oiled loaf pan, cover tightly with foil and leave at room temperature for 2-3 days. Cut in thin slices, wrap in foil and pack in lunch box. This makes a 3 lb/1.4 kg loaf, so if you wish you can halve the quantities.

COUNTRY SNACK

---

1 tablespoon honey	*2 oz/50 g chopped walnuts*
2 oz/50 g toasted almonds, finely chopped	*1 lb/450 g stoned dates*
1 oz/25 g candied peel, finely chopped	*Caster sugar*

It is best to buy whole dates and stone them yourself. Try and get nice big ones from a health food shop. Mix together all the other ingredients except the sugar and stuff the dates with the mixture. Roll in the sugar and store in an airtight tin. Wrap in foil to pack in lunch box.

SALMON FISHING — RIVERS IN THE SUMMER

My second introduction to fishing was on our honeymoon. Throughout our married life I only remember one week of holiday when we were not engaged in some sporting enterprise - honeymoons were no exception! On our way to Fishguard to catch the ferry to Ireland Archie had arranged for us to spend the night with an elderly cousin and his wife. No sooner had we arrived than I was flung in at the deep end, so to speak. Cousin Nugent thrust into my nerveless hands a spinning rod fitted with an antique Silex reel. Needless to say I spent most of the time undoing 'bird's nests' of nylon. When Cousin N took the rod it became a thing of beauty and the bait curved in a perfect parabola and landed exactly where he wanted, whereas in my hands it was invested with some evil spirit which usually made the bait land with a terrific splash, guaranteed to frighten any fish within miles. Although we did not catch anything that time, over the years we caught many fish from that pool. You only had to throw in your bait and you were almost certain to hook, if not land, a salmon. So pernickety was Cousin N that when it came to smoking a fish he stipulated that it must be a hen fish caught in April and weighing 22 pounds. Alas, his widow feels she is very lucky to get a fish at all, so much has the fishing deteriorated.

When we arrived in County Tipperary we discovered that there was a drought and that no one had caught a fish. Gloom and doom ensued. Luckily, on the culinary front there was unlimited butter, cream and steak, this at a time when there was still rationing in the United Kingdom. Archie, needless to say, being greedy, ate too much and suffered a bilious attack, which put him *hors de combat* for twenty-four hours! But on our last day he was fishing for trout with my little rod, with a tiny fly on, when suddenly, lo! and behold, he got into a salmon. It took an hour and a half to land, and then only by sheer luck as our ghillie kept dancing about on the bank saying 'Houly Mother of God' until, finally, he was persuaded to doff his boots and wade into the river and gaff it.

On our way back to catch the ferry at Rosslare we crossed a bridge with a perfect pool above it. This was too much for Archie so, as we had several hours to spare, we sought out the Garda and learned that the water was owned by the local Master of Foxhounds, whom we set out to find. We drove up a long avenue and came to a house with might easily have been the setting for a Molly Keane novel. After an age the bell was answered by a splendid figure in ancient tweed jacket with carpet slippers, one checked and one plain, followed by hounds and terriers. The library was festooned with cobwebs and dust, and stacked with papers so that there was literally not a chair to sit on. He was delighted for us to fish the pool, which we duly did but, sadly, unsuccessfuly. From all this you will have got some idea of Archie's commitment to sport — even honeymoons were not sacrosanct.

The kind of salmon river of which I am thinking is the equivalent of a Hampshire chalk-stream, and has well-equipped fishing huts and pools which are mostly within easy walking distance of a car. This makes your catering easier and you won't be confined to a haversack-type ration. I have noticed that where we fish on the Wye the fishing tenants usually have a good break for lunch, so a knife, fork and plate won't be spurned. Soup is always acceptable if the weather is chilly, and my goodness it can be in February and March. I am not so dedicated a fisher that I enjoy standing on a bank in a freezing east wind with hail or rain coming down and the line freezing in the rings, but most of the men I know are, so they will welcome a bit of inner warmth. If you are sending out a picnic for one or two you can pack any salad in individual plastic pots such as 8-oz/225-g yogurt containers, well washed out. You want to make everything as simple as possible. On the whole men don't have the patience to fiddle about with fancy wrappings, so, on a cold day, equip them with soup, some kind of main course, salad, cake and biscuits and scones for tea, plus a thermos so that the pangs of hunger can be assuaged before a long journey home.

Dabchick.

SOUPS

SPLIT PEA SOUP

This is an adaptable soup that can either be eaten with a spoon as a main course or thinned down and drunk. Either way it will raise morale.

---

1 lb/450 g dried green split peas	*1 teaspoon mixed herbs*
3 tablespoons fat bacon, finely minced	*1 tablespoon butter, creamed with 1*
1¼ pints/ 725 ml beef stock (can be	*teaspoon flour*
obtained fresh from Sainsbury's)	*1 teaspoon sugar*
2 pints/1 litre water	*Salt and pepper*

Serves 2-4

Soak the peas for 4 hours, drain and cook, covered, in 2 pints/1 litre salted water until tender. Strain and reserve the cooking liquid. Blend the peas in the Magimix until smooth. Sauté the bacon in a heavy pan, add all the cooking water and stock, peas, herbs, sugar and seasoning and simmer for 20 minutes. Stir in the butter and flour and cook for 5 minutes longer. If you are going along too take a packet of garlic croûtons to sprinkle in. Don't bother if he is going solo, as it's odds-on that the packet will remain unopened.

LEEK AND WATERCRESS SOUP

If watercress is not in season add some cress, finely chopped, or a little spinach. A handful of grated cheese makes the soup more substantial.

1 lb/450 g leeks, washed, trimmed and chopped	1 pint/575 ml milk
12 oz/350 g potatoes, peeled and cut up	1 tablespoon olive oil
1 bunch watercress or 1 container cress	1 teaspoon sugar
1 vegetable stock cube	4 oz/100 g grated cheese
1/4 pint/150 ml water	Salt and pepper

Serves 2-4

Cook the leek and potato in the oil over a low heat until it begins to look transparent, shaking so that it does not stick. Add the water, stock cube, sugar, salt and pepper and cook until soft. Liquidize in Magimix and add the milk. Re-heat and add the chopped watercress or cress and finally stir in the cheese.

RED POTTAGE

This vegetable soup came from an elderly relative's receipt book. The original recipe suggests that you boil the haricot beans with bicarbonate of soda, I suppose to eliminate their propellent qualities. I tried it out with tinned beans which saves time, and anyway I'm told that modern beans are treated in some way to prevent that airborne feeling.

1 tin haricot beans	2 pints/1 litre water
1 small tin tomato pulp	1 teaspoon sugar
12 oz/350 g beetroot, peeled and cut up	1 dessertspoon each chopped parsley and chives
8 oz/225 g onions, peeled and chopped	
4 oz/100 g parsnip, peeled and chopped	Salt and pepper

Serves 6-8

Put everything in a saucepan except the chopped herbs and simmer gently for 1 hour, or until tender. Process in the Magimix until creamy and smooth, re-heat and add parsley and chives. Nothing could be easier.

MAIN COURSES AND SALADS

A home-made Melton Mowbray pork pie is hard to beat, meltingly crisp pastry and tender, well-seasoned pork surrounded by delicious jelly. It is a different thing altogether from a bought one, although some of these can be excellent. They are not difficult to make, but you do need time so it is best to set aside a day for making pies and put any surplus in the freezer. It is also an excellent way of using up game. Archie loved a good pork pie and we used to try out all kinds of shop ones, but he was never happy until I started to make them myself. The first time I tried I was petrified, until I realised that it was just a terrine or pâté encased in pastry. The only thing you have to get right is the exact moment at which to start lining your mould. If the pastry's too hot it will slip down the sides and if too cold it will crack. Holes or splits in the pastry are fatal as the juices escape and the pie becomes soggy. Here is a good general-purpose recipe, and a few ideas for fillings. Once you have got the system under control you can experiment with different ingredients — veal, ham and egg; chicken and ham; turkey, ham, pork and cranberry. There is no end to the variations you can dream up.

BASIC HOT WATER CRUST

12 oz/350 g plain flour	¼ teaspoon salt
4 oz/100 g lard	1 dessertspoon icing sugar
¼ pint/150 ml (scant) water	1 egg, beaten

Sift together the flour, icing sugar and salt into a bowl and stand in a warm place. Melt the lard and water in a pan and bring to the boil, then pour into the flour and mix well with a wooden spoon. Turn onto a floured surface and knead until smooth. Use whilst still warm.

PORK PIE FILLING

Stock for Jelly
Bones from spareribs or shoulder of pork
2 pig's trotters
2 carrots
1 onion, unpeeled and stuck with cloves

1 celery stalk
1 bay leaf
6 black peppercorns
Salt

Cover with water and simmer for 4–5 hours. Strain and reduce to ½ pint/275 ml. Adjust seasoning, cool and skim fat off. This can be made the day before or, indeed, at any time previous to making the pie, in which case freeze it.

Filling
2 lbs/900 g boned shoulder or spareribs of pork, ⅓ fat to ⅔ lean (use bones for jelly)
8 oz/225 g thin, green streaky bacon rashers
1 teaspoon chopped sage

½ teaspoon each nutmeg, ground cloves and allspice
1 teaspoon green peppercorns
1 teaspoon anchovy essence
Salt and freshly ground black pepper

Serves 6-8

Chop half the pork and two of the bacon rashers. Mince the rest of the pork in the Magimix and then mix everything in a bowl. Fry a tiny knob of the mixture and taste, add more seasoning if necessary, remembering that flavours tend to disappear when cold.

To make the pie:

Roll out two-thirds of the pastry and line a hinged mould (you can get these from good ironmongers, or from Lakeland Plastics). An oblong tin produces something which is easier to slice but you can also use a round cake tin with detachable bottom and spring-clip slide. Lay the remaining rashers over the bottom and along the sides and fill with the pork mixture. Roll out the rest of the pastry, brush the edges of the pie with water, and cover with the rest of the pastry. Press together and decorate by pressing a fork round the edge. Cut a hole in the top and make a small funnel with rolled-up card pressed into the hole. Brush pie with beaten egg and bake in a pre-heated oven at 400°F/200°C/Gas Mark 6 for 30 minutes, then reduce the heat to 325°F/160°C/Gas mark 3 for a further 2 hours. Allow to cool, then remove the tin, brush the sides with beaten egg and return to the oven to brown, but lay a piece of foil on top to prevent it burning. Melt the jelly slightly so that it is cool but runny. Take out the paper funnel and pour jelly through hole. Leave to cool for 12 hours before eating.

TRICK OF THE TRADE: If you don't have or can't get a pig's trotter use the appropriate amount of aspic or gelatine in your stock.

GAME PIE FILLING

You will need 1½ lbs/675 g mixed game meat for this pie. To my mind it isn't a game pie unless it has at least three varieties of game. So many recipes just say hare or venison, for instance, in which case why not call it hare or venison pie? I know I am spoilt, as Archie and I were game dealers so we always had plenty of 'dodgy' or badly shot birds or beasts we could use. But even if you are not in the shooting world you can get quite a good selection from Sainsbury's, or you could track down your local game dealer. If you are in the shooting world, this is an excellent way of using up old or badly shot birds.

1 pheasant	Salt and ground black pepper
1 pigeon	
1 hare thigh	Marinade
1 lb/450 g stewing venison	½ pint/275 ml red wine
1 lb/450 g pork, half each of lean and fat	1 shallot, finely chopped
1 pig's trotter	1 carrot, finely chopped
8 oz/225 g thin streaky rashers of bacon	1 celery stalk, finely chopped
8 oz/225 g chestnut stuffing mix	2 bay leaves
1 teaspoon redcurrant or rowan jelly	1 teaspoon juniper berries
2 sprigs each of thyme and rosemary	6 black peppercorns

Serves 4-6

Cut the meat off the pheasant, pigeon and hare thigh and cover this and the venison with the marinade. Leave overnight in a covered dish in the fridge. Remove the meat and chop into small chunks. Put the carcasses, bones and pig's trotter into a saucepan with the marinade and water to cover. Simmer for 2 hours, strain and reduce to ¾ pint/425 ml. Soak the chestnut stuffing mix for 15 minutes in boiling water, mince the pork finely and mix thoroughly with the game meat, stuffing, redcurrant jelly, salt and pepper. Line a tin as in the basic recipe, lay bacon rashers on the bottom and round the sides, fill with the game mixture and on top lay the sprigs of rosemary and thyme, followed by the pastry 'top'. Cook as directed previously and pour in the jellied stock. Cool, then chill for 24 hours before eating.

PORTUGUESE CHICKEN PIE WITH PORT

Here is a completely different pie from Portugal which was given to me by a relation of Archie's who lived there for some years. We had to play around with the quantities as her cook just guessed the amounts, but this seems to work.

1 chicken weighing approx. 2½ lbs/1 kg	*1 teaspoon dried thyme*
or 6 chicken breasts	*1 bay leaf*
8 oz/225 g diced fat bacon	*1 oz/25 g butter*
8 oz/225 g small pickling onions, peeled	*1 oz/25 g flour*
but left whole	*¼ pint/150 ml stock (or ¼ stock cube and*
6 oz/175 g black olives, stoned	*water)*
6 oz/175 g mushrooms, finely chopped	*1 glass port*
3 garlic cloves, peeled and chopped	*1 small glass brandy*
1 dessertspoon parsley, chopped	*Salt and pepper*

Serves 4-6

Cut the chicken into pieces, or use breasts which makes it easier to eat. Place in a casserole with the garlic, thyme, bay leaf, parsley, salt and pepper and leave for 2 hours. Add the onions, make a roux with the butter and flour and add the stock and port and stir until smooth. Add the mushrooms and olives, cook for a few minutes and pour over the chicken pieces. Simmer very gently for 1 hour then add the brandy and cook for a further 15 minutes. Cool and refrigerate until the next day.

Pastry	*¾ pint/425 ml water*
	½ teaspoon salt
1 lb/450 g plain flour	*1 coffee spoon curry powder*
¾ pint/ 425 ml olive oil	

I see you pursing your lips and saying 'Tchk! Tchk! Funny ways these foreigners have, fancy using olive oil', but I promise you it works and is the Portuguese answer to a raised pie crust. Tip the oil into a bowl and add the warm water, whisking gently. The mixture should look smooth, rather white and light. Add the sieved flour and salt in small quantities.

Mix it all together quickly, make into a ball and let it rest for 1 hour. Roll out two-thirds of the pastry very thinly and line a well-greased 10-inch/25-cm cake tin with it. Place the chicken pieces on it, mounded in the centre, roll out the remaining pastry and cover. Seal the edges with water. Make two incisions in the top, brush with beaten egg and bake in a pre-heated oven at 400°F/200°C/Gas Mark 6 for 45 minutes. Cool and refrigerate.

SALADS

Make a small quantity of salad and put into a 8-oz/225-g Flora or yogurt pot with a lid. Tuck into the lidded plastic box in which you have put the pie.

---

1. Cherry tomatoes, halved, with a little good olive oil, a few drops of vinegar, salt, pepper, some crumbled feta cheese and bay leaves.

2. New potatoes, cut up whilst warm and dressed with oil, vinegar, salt and pepper with diced Spanish cabanos sausages, or pepperami.

3. Broccoli or calabrese lightly cooked in boiling, salted water so that it is still slightly crunchy or al dente. Dribble on a dressing made with hazelnut oil, lemon juice, salt and pepper and sprinkle on some toasted chopped hazelnuts.

4. Diced cold potato with chopped hard-boiled egg, spring onions and mayonnaise.

5. Tinned green flageolet beans with chopped onion, vinaigrette dressing and pine nut kernels.

6. Tiny cold new potatoes with bean sprouts tossed in a dressing made with sesame seed oil, vinegar, soy sauce and Lea & Perrins Ginger and Orange Sauce.

If you are sending your loved one out with pie and salad don't forget to include one or two generously buttered rolls or interesting bread. Cheese can be wrapped separately unless it is the gooey kind, in which case put it in one of the rolls. Don't forget knife, fork and spoon.

TEA

In the days when we first went up to stay with Archie's elderly cousin on the Wye there was a full complement of staff and, until the river washed it away, a splendid fishing hut. There, at a quarter to five exactly, the butler used to come down with a picnic basket of tea things. Nowadays few can rise to such heights of comfort, but what you can do is to provide a separate bag with a thermos of tea and a plastic box of sandwiches/scones/cakes. If the fishing is far away it will help to keep the wolf from the door before that long journey back.

SANDWICHES

These should be made with very thin bread and butter, crusts cut off and cut into four.

Suggestions: *Gentleman's Relish; egg and cress (plenty of filling so that your teeth sink in); cucumber; honey in granary bread. Even fish paste or chicken and ham paste can be delicious if spread thickly enough and well seasoned.*

CAKES

DODY'S SQUISHY CHOCOLATE CAKE

---

6 oz/175 g butter	*4 eggs*
4 oz/100 g self-raising flour	*6 oz/175 g drinking chocolate or cocoa*
4 oz/100 g caster sugar	*powder*

Serves 2–4

Cream the butter and sugar together in the Magimix and then add the eggs. Stop the machine and sieve in the flour and chocolate powder. Switch on and beat well. Oil a sandwich tin and pour in. Bake in a pre-heated oven at 350°F/175°C/Gas Mark 4 for 20 minutes. Do not overcook.

ORANGE AND NUT WHISKY CAKE

---

6 oz/175 g butter	*6 oz/175 g self-raising flour*
6 oz/175 g sugar	*6 oz/175 g seedless raisins*
3 egg yolks	*3 fl oz/80 ml whisky*
3 egg whites	*1 teaspoon grated orange peel*

Serves 4–6

Soak the raisins in the whisky overnight, then strain. Cream together the butter and sugar until light and fluffy, then break in the yolks one by one and beat well. Fold in the raisins, half the flour and the strained whisky. Beat the egg whites until stiff and fold in, together with the remaining flour. Turn into a buttered 7-inch/18-cm cake tin and bake in a pre-heated oven at 350°F/175°C/Gas Mark 4 for 1 hour. Cool and turn out. Split in half and spread with the filling (below).

4 oz/100 g icing sugar, sieved
1½ oz/40 g butter, softened

1 teaspoon grated orange peel
1 oz/25 g chopped walnuts
Whisky

Beat together the icing sugar and butter until light and creamy, add the orange peel and chopped nuts and enough whisky to flavour. Spread over the cake and sandwich halves together.

SALMON FISHING —
ICY CONDITIONS

WARMING FOOD

Archie always said his coldest fishing expedition was to the Dee one March. He was on a beat that could only be fished from a boat, which meant that the wretched ghillie was on the bank letting the boat drift down on the end of a rope, while Archie sat motionless in the driving sleet, snow and hail. When they stopped for lunch (fortunately there was a fishing hut) neither of them could open the sandwich box as they practically had frostbite. Luckily Archie had a bottle of whisky which they downed between them. He said it had absolutely no effect and did not make them in the least drunk. The only compensation was that during the afternoon they landed a fish. It just goes to show that my theory is right — all fanatical fishermen/sportsmen are mad.

There are generally fishing huts with benches and tables on the larger salmon rivers, so you can send a wide-mouthed thermos containing a thick soup or even a stew, as well as a plastic bowl and spoon.

CLASSIC HARIRA WITH LENTILS

This is the national soup of Morocco, and during Ramadan it is the first food to be taken after sunset. I went to Marrakesh last year with Lucy's godmother, who is over eighty, and we had some hilarious times. One episode in particular stands out. When we decided to visit the souk, we were verbally assailed from all sides by aggressive touts and would-be guides as we got out of the taxi. Auntie Constance wasn't having any nonsense, however, so she laid about her with her umbrella, saying in a loud voice '*Imshi! Imshi!*', which is Arabic for '.... off'! They were so taken aback that we were left in peace. I got this recipe from our regular guide, Achmed.

8 oz/225 g lean lamb cut into ½-inch/2-cm dice	*¼ teaspoon black pepper*
3 or 4 small bones, lightly grilled	*½ teaspoon saffron*
8 oz/225 g small onions	*½ oz/25 g butter*
2 pints/1 litre water	*4 oz/100 g lentils cooked in salted water and drained*

Serves 6-8

Simmer all the ingredients except the lentils, which should have the juice of 1 lemon squeezed over them when you have drained them. Remove the onions from the stock when they are tender and put to one side. Continue cooking the bouillon until the meat is tender, about 1 hour, then remove the bones and add:

1 tube or tin of concentrated tomato purée	*1 oz/25 g butter*
1 dessertspoon chopped parsley	*1 oz/25 g flour*
1 dessertspoon chopped coriander	*Salt and pepper*
1 tablespoon lemon juice	

Melt the butter and sprinkle in the flour, add some of the bouillon and stir until it thickens, and then add the rest of it and all the other ingredients, including the onions and lentils. Season well. Achmed gave me a recipe for twelve people, as of course his quantities were for a large Moroccan family, but I have adapted it. You can add a little more water if it seems too thick. Cut down on the lemon juice if it is too tart and add a little sugar. Instead of lentils you can use chickpeas and broad beans, and substitute chicken for the lamb.

CHOWDERS

These are excellent thick soupy stews from New England. Most people might have the idea that they are only made with clams, as that is one of the more famous versions, but Corn Chowder and Fish Chowder made with smoked haddock are quite delicious, although it is as well to know that your fisherman likes to eat fish as well as catch it before you send him out with a brimming thermos of the stuff.

CORN CHOWDER

1 oz/25 g salt pork, diced	½ pint/275 ml boiling water
4 oz/100 g onion, chopped	1½ pints/850 ml milk
2 oz/50 g butter	8 oz/225 g mashed potatoes
12 oz/350 g whole corn kernels	Salt and pepper

Serves 6-8

Sauté the pork and onions until they are golden, then add the corn and water and cook for 10 minutes. Add milk, potato and seasoning and heat through thoroughly. A really quick soup, and if you don't happen to have salt pork just use any kind of bacon.

SMOKED HADDOCK CHOWDER

You don't have to use smoked haddock — any white fish such as cod, whiting or plain haddock will do — but something smoked is best.

4 oz/100 g fat salt pork or fat bacon, diced	Black pepper tea (made by simmering 1
1 large onion, sliced	tablespoon black peppercorns in ¼
1 oz/25 g butter	pint/150 ml water until flavour is
1 lb/450 g potatoes, peeled and sliced	extracted)
1½ lbs/675 g smoked haddock (preferably	1 bay leaf
finnan haddock), skinned and diced	Paprika
1½ pints/850 ml milk	Salt
½ pint/275 ml water	1 tablespoon grated cheese (optional)

Serves 4-6

Brown the bacon and onion in the butter in a heavy pan, cover and simmer until onions are transparent, then add potatoes and water to pan, as well as the paprika, salt, bay leaf and pepper tea. When potatoes are done add milk and fish and cook for a further 10 minutes. It is not traditional, but I add a tablespoonful of grated cheese.

PORK AND BEANS

Still on the American wavelength is this warming bean casserole, which can be adapted in many ways. Here is a classic version. Don't cheat with tinned baked beans unless you have to, it's really quite easy with dried beans nowadays.

8 oz/225 g dried haricot or kidney beans	1 dessertspoon made American mustard
8 oz/225 g salt pork, diced	(Colman's)
8 oz/225 g onion, chopped	Water
1 tablespoon black treacle	Salt and pepper

Serves 2-4

Wash the beans several times and leave to soak overnight. Cook in the soaking water with the pork and onion for 2-3 hours with 1 teaspoon salt. Add the rest of the ingredients, mixed with a little water, and bake in a pre-heated oven at 300°F/150°C/Gas Mark 2 for 3 hours. If too thick add a little more water mixed with half a ham stock cube.

CAKES AND SCONES

A hefty cheese bap is just the thing to go with any of these main-course soups, and for something sweet a good slab of North Country cake or some kind of scone and jam. The weather that I am writing about will not make you long for cooling fruit or salads, just plain honest-to-goodness filling fare. Forget about cholesterol and losing weight, the wind-chill factor will soon put paid to such thoughts.

MRS VI DAVIES'S YORKSHIRE PARKIN

This recipe was given to me by the mother of a friend of mine. The much-thumbed exercise book which she lent me was a positive gold mine of old-fashioned cake and bread recipes.

4 oz/100 g self-raising flour	1 egg
4 oz/100 g medium oatmeal	4 level tablespoons golden syrup
2 oz/50 g brown sugar	1 level tablespoon black treacle
1 level teaspoon ground ginger	1½ oz/40 g lard
¼ teaspoon bicarbonate of soda	1 tablespoon milk
1 pinch salt	

Mix all the dry ingredients together, except the sugar. Melt lard, sugar, syrup, treacle and a little of the milk. Beat the egg and add to the dry ingredients along with the melted lard etc. Tip into a greased tin 9 inches/23 cm x 9 inches/23 cm and bake in a pre-heated oven at 300°F/150°C/Gas Mark 2 for 1 hour 20 minutes.

MRS VI DAVIES'S WALNUT BREAD

5 oz/150 g self-raising flour	½ oz/15 g lard
3 oz/75 g granulated sugar	1 level tablespoon golden syrup
¼ teaspoon bicarbonate of soda	8 tablespoons milk
1 oz/25 g walnuts	1 egg
1 oz/25 g sultanas	1 pinch salt
½ oz/15 g margarine	

Sieve the flour, bicarbonate of soda and salt into the Magimix, add the fat cut into small pieces and blend for a few seconds. Pour in the milk, well-beaten egg and treacle and beat well. Sprinkle in the walnuts and sultanas and give a few short bursts to mix. Bake in a greased tin in a pre-heated oven at 325°F/160°C/Gas Mark 3 for 1¼ hours.

MRS VI DAVIES'S MALT BREAD

6 oz/175 g wholemeal flour	1½ teaspoons bicarbonate of soda
6 oz/175 g white self-raising flour	4 oz/100g mixed dried fruit
3 oz/75 g dark brown Muscovado sugar	½-¾ pint/275 ml-425 ml milk
3 large tablespoons malt extract	1 pinch salt

Sift the two flours, bicarbonate of soda and salt into a bowl. Warm the malt, milk and sugar, add to the flour and mix all together. Stir in the mixed fruit and spoon into a greased 1½-pint/850-ml loaf tin and bake in a pre-heated oven at 325°F/160°C/Gas Mark 3 for 1¼ hours. turn out onto a wire rack and leave to cool. Wrap in foil and leave for at least two days before eating. For your fisherman's picnic serve sliced, spread with butter or cream cheese and sandwiched together.

POTATO SCONES

You need to use a really floury potato for this such as Pentland Squire or Maris Piper.

---

*12 oz/350 g freshly cooked potato, well
mashed
2 oz/50 g softened butter*

*3 oz/75 g flour
Salt*

Beat the butter, flour and salt into the mashed potatoes. Roll out thinly on a floured surface. Cut into rounds and bake on a greased baking sheet in a pre-heated oven at 425°F/220°C/Gas Mark 7 for 20 minutes. Cool, then butter generously and sandwich together with jam.

CATERING FOR FISHING HOLIDAYS

In the thirty-seven years that I was married to Archie I had to cater and cope in some pretty peculiar places, and was always expected to turn out something passable, if not exactly *haute cuisine*. He never thought twice about asking our host/landlord and family to supper. No matter that there were only plates and cutlery for four and three chairs to sit on, he was always optimistic and expected me to manage.

The expedition that sticks in my mind is one we took to the Isle of Lewis. We crossed to Skye on a Sunday, not having booked a bed as Archie had said, in his usual airy-fairy way, 'Oh! we'll easily find a B&B'. We arrived at Kyleakin at six o'clock expecting that round the next bend we would see a nice B&B sign, but every one we came to was draped with a sack. Finally, very dispirited, we got to Portree thinking that even if we couldn't get a bed at least we would be able to get supper. Not a hope — all we were able to find was a warmed-up pie off a stall. Eventually, at the last house we came to, we asked the lady if she knew anywhere we could spend the night and she said she thought the English lady would take us. So off we set up a very small road and stopped at the only dwelling we could see. Success at last! We were directed to 'the caravan at the bottom of the garden', which turned out to be a pukka gypsy caravan, gaily painted and full of rustic charm including real live fleas and midges. The dearth of B&B facilities was explained by the fact that Skye is strong on the Wee Free and they don't hold with commerce on the Sabbath.

Finally we arrived at our destination, a superbly luxurious converted shooting lodge where we were to spend a week as paying guests, although thereafter Archie rented (sight unseen the first time) a deserted keeper's cottage. This was a bit of a come-down after the pampered time we had spent at 'the big hoose', but it had its compensations, one of them being the loo, which was situated at the bottom of the garden in a bower of rowan trees just above a burn (instant, if unecological, sewage disposal). It had no door and you looked away down a little glen to the sea loch. There were all kinds of birds, and it was a great temptation to stay there all morning.

The big disadvantage of the cottage was that it was haunted. Lucy slept in the attic and was unaffected, but our room, which was off the living room/kitchen, had a dreadful feel to it. Neither of the dogs would cross the threshold and their hackles rose as soon as they got near the door. When we went to bed we each felt as if an iron band had been clamped round our foreheads, and twice we woke to see a disembodied head shining brightly and hovering above us. Archie claimed to have seen the 'little people' and told them that we wouldn't harm them so would they please leave us alone. I can see all you sceptics saying that we had drunk too much whisky, but I can only say that I have never been anywhere like it before or since.

There was no electricity and so we were lit by paraffin and candles, and cooked on a tiny kitchen range. I'm afraid to say that with Archie's propensity for fishing until the last possible moment, I became very idle and resorted mostly to the frying-pan. Stornaway was forty miles away and the village shop only had eggs, butter, tinned peas, bacon and bread. There was no 'longlife' milk, so Archie had a feast of sweetened condensed milk. It is the only time I have become quite sick of sea trout, which was our staple diet; we had it fried, cold with mayonnaise (which had to be made with frying oil as olive oil was unknown in those parts), and in fishcakes, kedgeree, chowder, and a sort of rough pâté.

All this was fifteen years ago, and I expect holiday cottages are better equipped nowadays. Even in the farthest-flung villages and towns you can get a surprising number of speciality foods, but it is best to take some standbys to tide you over any lapses of memory with the shopping list. You don't want to have to trail twenty-five miles or more to get milk or bread. Soda bread is easy to make, and with home-made scones and oatcakes you hardly need to bother with a baker. A Magimix or food-processor isn't as much of a luxury as you think and will save hours of time, as well as enabling you to have some really gourmet dishes. Do beware, though, and take a selection of adaptors — in many parts of Scotland they haven't heard of the ring-main system and square-pin plugs, so you may find yourself literally trying to put a square pin into a round hole. I have made a check list of things I would take, but have not included fishing tackle, which I consider to be the domain of your fishing partner.

You may have your own ideas and priorities, but set out below is what I would choose myself. You don't want to spend hours slaving over the stove — this is, after all, your holiday too — so short-cuts and tricks of the trade are all important. It is hardly likely that you will want to spend hours making stock, so just use stock cubes or some kind of tinned consommé where a recipe calls for it. You may wonder why I have included a thick frying-pan and a casserole. Bitter experience has shown me that the catering equipment of holiday 'lets' usually comprises two or three battered aluminium saucepans, a thin-based frying-pan that has been burnt several times and won't therefore sit flat on the cooker, and a small and inadequate Pyrex casserole.

CHECK LIST
COOK'S EQUIPMENT
Sharp knives, including cook's knife which can double as carving/bread knife, your favourite paring knife and a filleting knife
Knife sharpener
Heavy frying-pan
Cast-iron enamelled casserole
Magimix or similar food-processor
Electric hand-beaters (optional). Very useful and they don't take up much room
Chopping board. Even a small one is invaluable. Countless times I have searched in vain on arriving at our holiday cottage to find that the only thing to chop on is the small round bread board, which you want to use for bread anyway
Tin-openers and corkscrews are usually provided, but if you have a favourite one, take it
Lidded plastic lunch-boxes x number of guests plus some extra for the spur-of-the-moment invitee
2 or more large thermos flasks
Cold-box and/or insulated bag
Paper plates, napkins, cups, plastic cutlery. Optional, and only if you are desperate to cut down on washing-up. But unecological
HERBS
Herbes de Provence or Italian mixed herbs, dried basil, dill weed, thyme, oregano, juniper berries, coriander seed, bay leaves, garlic cloves
SPICES
Garlic and lemon pepper, curry powder, nutmeg, celery salt, *wooden pepper mill* and black peppercorns, Dijon mustard

SAUCES

Catering-size jar Hellman's mayonnaise, large bottle good olive oil, wine vinegar, tubes tomato purée, soy sauce, Lea & Perrins Ginger and Orange Sauce, tabasco, Worcester Sauce, Green Label Mango Chutney, tomato ketchup, horseradish sauce, apple sauce

PRESERVES TO ACCOMPANY, AND FOR USE IN, COOKED DISHES

Rowan, redcurrant, or cranberry jelly

TINNED VEGETABLES

Petit pois, sweet corn, green flageolet beans, spinach, haricot/kidney beans, button mushrooms, tinned/bottled beets

TINNED SOUPS

Oxtail, beef and chicken consommé, cream of mushroom, cream of chicken, Campbell's Indonesian Vegetable Soup

TINNED FRUIT

Raspberries/loganberries, strawberries, blackcurrants. Plus any others of your choice, but these three will make an easy summer pudding.

STOCK CUBES

Chicken, beef, ham, pork, fish, vegetable. All or some according to your whim

DRIED GOODS AND CEREALS

Lentils, tagliatelle, basmati or pilau rice, medium and coarse oatmeal. You shouldn't have any difficulty getting the latter in Scotland, anyway, but don't forget it. Wholemeal flour, strong white flour, bicarbonate of soda, cream of tartar and baking powder for soda bread

DRIED FRUIT

Dried apricots, seedless raisins, dates

SOUPS

As long as you are equipped with onions, potatoes, garlic, milk, stock cubes and the above-mentioned tins, you should be able to rustle up an interesting soup in no time at all. Be on the look-out, though, for you never know what you may find.

On our last Scottish fishing trip before Archie died we rented a 'mobile home' on the shores of Loch Awe. It was honestly the cosiest 'butt and ben' I can ever remember holidaying in — bedroom, bathroom, shower, loo, dining room/bedroom, sink, sitting room, telly and gas fire. The view was stupendous, right over the loch to Ben Cruachan, and the water lapping away just below us. The great plus was that a mass of wild sorrel grew in profusion all around us, so I made a delicious sorrel soup. The farmer's wife thought we were quite mad picking and eating weeds, as she put it.

WILD SORREL SOUP

8 oz/225 g potatoes, peeled and cut up	½ chicken stock cube
1 onion, peeled and cut up	½ pint/275 ml water
1 oz/25 g butter	½ pint/275 ml milk
2 good handfuls sorrel, washed and chopped roughly	1 teaspoon sugar
	Salt and pepper

Serves 2-4

Cook the potatoes and onion in the butter until transparent, add the chopped sorrel and shake, pour in the water, stock cube and seasoning and cook until tender, about 15 minutes, sugar and seasoning then blend in the Magimix. If no Magimix, just pulp well with a potato masher, then thin down to required consistency with milk. It won't be so elegant, but will taste just as good.

CHANTERELLE SOUP

When Lucy was about five Archie was invited to fish on the Spey with some people we didn't know very well. We had to take her with us, and were a bit worried about how she would fit in. We needn't have bothered, for our hostess was a most unusual person. Not only was she an ace labrador trainer and field-trialer, but she also had a PhD in Botany. Her speciality was fungi, and we used to go for wonderful forays, bringing back baskets of them for identification. Sadly, at that time people weren't 'into' wild mushrooms for eating and we just threw them away after naming them.

Years later we rented a cottage by the Dee, in a place where all kinds of wild mushrooms grew. People would slink furtively up the drive of the big house with sacks which, once filled, they put on the plane to London where they fetched vast prices. By this time I at least knew what a chanterelle looked like — an orange parasol blown inside-out — and there were masses of them in the birch woods nearby. I knew that Archie and our guests would never eat 'fungi', so I just pretended that it was mushroom soup, at least until they had sampled it and said how delicious it was.

---

1 lb/450 g chanterelle mushrooms, washed and finely chopped	*1 pint/575 ml milk*
1 onion, peeled and finely chopped	*1 dessertspoon cornflour mixed with a little milk*
1 clove garlic, finely chopped	*1 can mushroom soup made up to 1*
2 oz/50 g butter or 2 tablespoons oil	*pint/575 ml with milk*
1 chicken stock cube	*Salt and pepper*

Serves 2-4

Cook the chanterelles, onions, and garlic in the butter or oil until tender, shaking occasionally. Add the milk, stock cube and cornflour and bring to the boil, stirring constantly until it thickens, or simply tip in the can of soup and the milk and season. Really scrummy, so don't be cowardly, chanterelles are one of the easiest wild mushrooms to identify.

MOULES MARINIÈRE

One of Archie's brothers lived on the Argyll coast. His land included a beautiful wild bay edged with rocks, and at low tide there were thousands of mussels. Lucy and I gathered some and then announced our intention of making Moules Marinière. The family were quite horrified, and thought we were mad. At supper time they couldn't resist coming down to see if we were dead or not, and believed that each delicious mouthful would be our last.

---

4 pints/2.3 litres mussels	1 pinch dried thyme
½ pint/275 ml dry white wine	1 dessertspoon fresh parsley, (chopped if
4 shallots or 1 onion, peeled and chopped	available)
very finely	Pepper but no salt
1 clove garlic, peeled and finely chopped	

Serves 2-4

Wash the mussels in several lots of clean water and scrub the shells as well as possible. Place in a large saucepan with all the other ingredients and cook, covered, over a high heat for about 6-10 minutes or until the shells have opened. Discard those that are not opened. Fish the rest out, put them in a dish and keep warm. Strain the cooking liquid through a tea-towel to get rid of the sand and grit and tip into a clean saucepan, add some more chopped onion and garlic (optional) and parsley and cook for a further 10 minutes. You can add cream if you wish, but I think the sauce is much nicer *au nature*.

NETTLE SOUP

This is another much-neglected and delicious what-I-call 'freebie' soup, but do wear thick gloves and cover your arms when picking the nettles.

---

2 pints/1 litre young nettle shoots	a stock cube
1 onion, peeled and finely chopped	2 tablespoons fine or medium oatmeal
4 oz/100 g butter	Salt and pepper
2 pints/1 litre stock, or water and	Sugar

Serves 4-6

Cook the onions in the butter until tender and transparent, add the nettle shoots, stock and seasonings and bring to the boil, sprinkle in the oatmeal and simmer for 15 minutes. Adjust seasoning if necessary; it may need a little sugar.

TURNIP SOUP

This is also excellent made with swede (see *Prue's Perfect Guide to the Shoot Lunch*). Fresh vegetables are always a bit of a problem in Scotland, as in out-of-the-way places they are both expensive and scarce, and the choice is pretty limited. Root vegetables are nearly always available, however, so it's wise to make the best of what is on offer; so, if there are no turnips, then use swedes or even parsnips.

1 lb/450 g turnips, peeled and cut up	*1 oz/25 g butter*
1 pint/575 ml chicken stock or 1 can	*1 teaspoon sugar*
chicken consommé and water	*1 pinch ground nutmeg*
½ pint cream (optional), or milk	*Salt and pepper*
1 egg yolk	

Serves 2-4

Cook the turnips in the stock with the butter, sugar and seasoning until tender, then mash or process in the Magimix. Beat the egg yolks with a little milk and whisk into the soup. Re-heat but do not boil. If you don't want to use cream, use milk.

QUICK CONSOMMÉ AND CREAM CHEESE

1 tin Campbell's condensed consommé	*1 clove garlic, peeled and finely chopped*
8 oz/225 g cream cheese	*Fresh parsley, chopped, if available*

Serves 2
Whizz everything together and heat through.

There are all kinds of combinations you can try which will save time and taste more interesting if you tart them up a bit. For instance:

Spinach and cream of chicken or cream of chicken with chopped spring onion, a pinch of dried ginger and a dash of soy sauce.

Campbell's Indonesian Vegetable Soup with a dessertspoonful of peanut butter and a dash of Lea & Perrins Lime and Chillie Sauce.

TRICK OF THE TRADE: If cream is difficult to get, try using cream cheese diluted with a little milk, but add a suspicion of sugar to offset any tartness.

MAIN COURSES

I know that this is supposed to be a book about picnics, but if you are away on a self-catering holiday very often you can organize your menu so that you can make use of your main supper course for packed lunches on the next day. Simplicity is the watchword, so if you are sharing with other friends and they ask what they should bring, ask for a whole cooked ham and/or turkey. This gives you at least one if not two possibilities for trouble-free lunches. With any luck you should catch some fish, so this takes care of another day's menu. Breakfast is another useful source of bap fodder as you can just cook extra sausages/bacon/eggs or whatever and stuff them in baps or rolls.

TURKEY AND SAUSAGEMEAT PIE

This recipe was given me by a friend whose husband is a wildlife cameraman for the BBC. It is apparently much in favour with him and his colleagues when they have been deep-sea diving. The quantities are for 10 people so it does admirably for supper for 4 and then the next day in a lunch pack.

Filling

1½ lbs/675 g raw turkey, chicken or pork
cut into 1-in/3-cm cubes
1 lb/450 g sausagemeat
1 tablespoon Worcester Sauce
1 heaped teaspoon thyme
1 pinch dried rosemary, crumbled up finely
Salt and ground black pepper

Topping

3 tablespoons water

1 tablespoon gelatine
1 tablespoon Worcester Sauce
½ pint/275 ml dry cider
2 hard-boiled eggs
1 tablespoon chopped parsley

Pastry

10 oz plain flour
½ teaspoon salt
6 tablespoons cooking oil
5 tablespoons water
1 tablespoon Worcester Sauce

Serves 8–10

Sift the flour and salt into a bowl. Heat the oil, water and Worcester Sauce until it is bubbling, and then pour into the bowl. Mix well with a knife and when cool enough turn onto a floured surface and knead until smooth. Roll out to a 9-inch/23-cm x 14-inch/35½-cm oblong and fold in three. Lift into a 2-lb/900-g loaf tin or collapsible tin. Unfold the pastry and press into the tin, firming it well into the corners. Ease it up the sides so that there is ½ inch/2 cm hanging over the edge, then fold this in and crimp round with a fork to make a tidy ledge.

Mix the filling ingredients all together and press into the pie. Bake in a pre-heated oven at 475°F/240°C/Gas Mark 9 for 30 minutes and then reduce to 300°F/150°C/Gas Mark 2 for 1½ hours, then remove from oven and allow to cool completely. Dissolve the gelatine in the water, cider and Worcester Sauce and allow to cool. Arrange the hard-boiled eggs over the top, pour over the glaze and sprinkle with parsley.

Variation: Instead of the hard-boiled egg spread cooked cranberries over the top of the pie and then glaze, or decorate with lightly cooked slices of apple. If you do this, use apples that won't go fluffy when stewed.

CHICKEN LIVER LOAF

This is a really easy kind of French 'meat-loaf-with-a-difference' which can be made with an ordinary meat mincer and cooked in a cake tin.

10 oz/300 g chicken, calf's or pig's liver	*2 dessertspoons brandy*
8 oz/225 g white bread, without crusts	*1 dessertspoon parsley, chopped*
Milk	*1 pinch each ground nutmeg, cloves,*
1 small onion, peeled and finely chopped	*cayenne*
1 clove garlic, peeled and finely chopped	*Salt and ground black pepper*
3 eggs	

Serves 4-6

Soak the bread in the milk until it swells and then squeeze out the excess liquid. Cut up the livers and put through a meat mincer alternately with the bread, or put the bread and livers in the Magimix and process in sharp bursts so that it is not too finely ground. Then add the onion, garlic, parsley and seasonings, brandy, and finally the eggs, one by one. Make sure it is very well seasoned. Butter an oblong cake tin liberally, fill with the mixture and cook in a pre-heated oven at 375°F/190°C/Gas Mark 5 for about 1 hour. Test with a skewer and press gently. If the resulting juice is red cook for a little longer or until it runs clear. Turn out when it is almost cold. Serve with a lemon mayonnaise made with 2 egg yolks, 1 teaspoon mild Dijon mustard, salt, pepper, olive oil and lemon juice. Just before serving fold in the finely grated zest of 1 lemon and the whites of the eggs, stiffly beaten. Use for lunch the next day cut in thick slices as a sandwich.

OTHER IDEAS FOR SANDWICHES

Finely chopped cold lamb mixed with redcurrant or mint jelly and chopped toasted hazelnuts.

Cold trout mashed up with horseradish sauce, mayonnaise and chopped almonds.

Tinned shrimps mixed with Hellman's mayonnaise, chopped spring onion (or a little ordinary onion), a little grated carrot, a pinch of dried ground ginger and a dash of soy sauce.

BREAD, SCONES, CAKES, ETC.

You don't want to spend precious fishing time slaving over the stove making complicated puddings, so I will just suggest that you plump for fruit, cheese, milk puddings, with perhaps a summer pudding made from fresh or tinned raspberries, blackcurrants and strawberries, or a mixture. Tarts are quite easy to run up if you have the Magimix so I include a variation on a treacle tart.

TREACLE TART WITH GINGER AND WALNUTS

This should really be made with treacle and the syrup from preserved stem ginger, but you will hardly want to lug this with you just for one dish, so compromise with dried ginger mixed with warmed golden syrup.

6 oz/175 g plain flour	*6 tablespoons golden syrup*
4 oz/100 g butter	*2 oz/50 g chopped walnuts*
1-2 tablespoons water	*½ teaspoon dried ground ginger*
Pinch salt	*1 egg beaten with 1 tablespoon water*
2 oz/50 g white breadcrumbs	

Serves 4-6

Sift the flour and salt into the Magimix and add the butter cut into small pieces. Process for 15 seconds or until it is like fine breadcrumbs, or rub in by hand. Add the water and mix until it forms a ball. Cover in cling-film and put in fridge for half an hour. Roll out pastry, and line a buttered 8-inch/20-cm flan dish or cake tin. Cut off the overhang and re-roll. Sprinkle in the breadcrumbs and smooth them down. Warm the syrup so that it is runny but not hot. Dissolve the ginger in a little hot water and add to the syrup, stir well and pour over the breadcrumbs, then sprinkle over the nuts. Wet the rim of the pastry and make a lattice pattern with strips of the remaining pastry and brush with the beaten egg. (Omit the lattice bit if, like me, you find it a chore.) Bake in a pre-heated oven at 400°F/200°C/Gas Mark 6 for 12 minutes, then reduce to 350°F/175°C/Gas Mark 4 for 20-25 minutes.

SODA BREAD

This is so good that you may be inspired to make a weekly batch. It is the better for keeping and there are quite a lot of variations; also, as there is no yeast involved, you don't have the fag of waiting for it to rise. Another big plus is the fact that if, by any remote chance, your holiday accommodation does not have an oven, you can make it with a girdle, that is, the big thick, cast-iron frying-pan that you have had the forethought to bring with you.

1 lb 6 oz/650 g wholemeal flour	2 level teaspoons bicarbonate of soda
10 oz/300 g strong white flour	2 level teaspoons sugar
2 oz/50 g oatmeal	4 level teaspoons cream of tartar
2 level teaspoons salt	1½ pints/850 ml half milk, half water

Put all the dry ingredients into a large bowl and mix well. Add enough liquid to make a soft dough. Turn onto a floured surface and shape into a large round. Place on a greased baking tray and cut into four or six. Bake in a pre-heated oven at 450°F/230°C/Gas Mark 4 for a further 20-30 minutes, or until the loaf sounds hollow when tapped.
Variation: To make a change you can mix in a handful of dried fruit, chopped walnuts, hazelnuts, or chopped stoned dates.

WELSH CAKES

This came from the recipe book of the redoubtable Sophy, who presided over the pre-war kitchen of Cousin Nugent's house on the Welsh borders.

8 oz/225 g self-raising flour	3 oz/75 g caster sugar
1½ oz/40 g butter	1 egg
1½ oz/40 g lard	Milk
3 oz/75 g currants	

Rub the butter and lard into the flour, or process in the Magimix. Add the currants, sugar, and enough milk to make a stiff dough. Roll out ¼-inch/1-cm thick and cut into rounds (a fluted cutter is traditional), and bake on a girdle over a medium heat for 3 minutes on each side or until golden brown. Cool on a wire rack and dust with sugar before serving.

POTATO SCONES

You can eat these hot with butter (deliciously fattening), or cold with jam in a lunch pack. Any left over can be fried-up for breakfast. Very filling.

1½ lbs/675 g boiled potatoes (Pentland Squire or Maris Piper are good floury varieties)

1 oz/25 g butter
6 oz/175 g plain flour
1 teaspoon salt

Best made with freshly boiled potatoes, though you can use left-over ones if you warm them up again. Mash well with the salt and butter and then add the flour to make a stiff dough. Roll out ¼-inch/1-cm thick and cut into approximately 8-inch/20-cm rounds and then cut into four or six. Cook on a girdle over a medium heat for about 5 minutes on each side.

SCOTCH PANCAKES

This was one of Archie's old nanny's specialities. Never a person for the weighing scales, it suited her to measure things by the spoonful, or, as she used to say in a maddening way, 'by eye'.

6 rounded tablespoons plain flour
2 level teaspoons sugar
½ teaspoon cream of tartar
¼ teaspoon baking powder

1 egg, well beaten
¼ pint milk
1 pinch salt

Sieve all the dry ingredients into a bowl. Add the egg and milk to make a fairly thick batter of about the consistency of thick cream. Heat the girdle or frying-pan, grease well and drop spoonfuls of batter onto it. After about 3 minutes bubbles will start to rise, at which point turn and cook for a further 2-3 minutes. Delicious hot with butter, or cold for lunch made into a sandwich with butter, cheese and jelly.

CAMPING AND BARBECUES

Archie and I camped a lot very early on in our marriage, not only for weekends of pigeon shooting but also for fishing holidays. Even the humblest of B&Bs was beyond our means and if friends could not put us up it was Hobson's choice and we had to camp. In the beginning we didn't even have a tent, just a groundsheet and sleeping-bags. Our cooking equipment was minimal — a kettle, a frying-pan, two mugs, two forks, two spoons and two pocket knives, and a tin-opener for the inevitable standby of baked beans. We had a very primitive camping stove fuelled by solid meths blocks, one of which just about lasted long enough to boil a kettle. Generally we cooked over a real fire.

Finally we got a tent and christened it by going to camp on the banks of the Upper Wye at Doldowlod, which belonged to David and Di Gibson-Watt. He was a Member of Parliament and we went there just before the Coronation, for which they had seats. Our *quid pro quo* for being able to fish this beautiful bit of river was a request that we catch a salmon for a dinner party they were giving on Coronation night. The river was really low, and gloom and doom increased as there was no sign of a fish. We tried everything from early morn until dusk. Finally — and I regret to say this — Archie managed to 'sniggle' a salmon from the Rock Pool with a triangle. We rushed up to the house and Phillips, the chauffeur, drove at breakneck speed up to London where he, and the fish, arrived in the nick of time for it to be cooked for the dinner party. I don't know if David realises to this day how his 'Coronation' salmon was caught.

Nowadays, with four-wheel-drive vehicles and estate cars, it is all much easier, but we had to cram everything into an old snub-nosed Austin 10, known endearingly as 'BWO'. She did us proud, and if only we had been able to retire her gracefully in moth-balls no doubt she would now be worth a fortune as a collector's piece. For two people, as far as I am concerned, the simpler the better is my motto. The less clobber you take the less you'll have to worry about. My check list is just for the catering side of things; there is such a huge variety of actual camping equipment that it is really a case of personal choice and how much you are prepared to spend. Just include a minimum of herbs and spices. It is surprising how you can transform even the humble baked bean with a touch of this or that.

CHECK LIST
1 x 2-burner Calor Gas cooker with 3.9-kg canister
1 special spanner for tightening the nuts so that the gas doesn't leak
1 non-stick frying-pan
1 enamel milk saucepan
1 kettle
1 palette knife
1 wooden spoon
1 all-purpose cook's knife or folding hunting knife
1 sharpener or stone
Cutlery, mugs, and plates for 2
1 tin-opener
1 corkscrew
1 or 2 thermos flasks
Washing-up liquid, pan scourer, pan brush
Plenty of thick-quality kitchen paper, this is one occasion you really need it
Small bottle of Worcester Sauce
Mixed herbs
Seasoned pepper
Seasoned salt
Garlic powder
Stock cubes
Salt
Sugar
Tins baked beans, soup
Medium or pinhead oatmeal
Butter, bacon, tea/coffee, sausages, bread, Long Life milk

I have listed a 2-burner Calor Gas cooker as it's quite a bore not to be able to boil a kettle at the same time as cooking supper, but if you want to cut down just take a small gas cooker with a large supply of the little canisters (but do make sure you throw the empties in a litter bin). These little stoves are quite handy as you can get a lamp fitment which screws in easily and gives you some light by which to do the washing-up.

When we were staying on the island of Lewis, Archie and Lucy left me in the haunted cottage for a night whilst they went on an overnight camping expedition to a very inaccessible loch with the keeper and our host's daughter. No mod. cons. such as Land-Rovers, just a hill pony to carry the tents, and everything else in knapsacks. The fishing was not very successful and they only caught one trout, which was left on a flat rock ready for breakfast the next morning. The midges were so terrible that they all resorted to wearing tights over their heads for protection, which made them look like outlandish terrorists. In order to get some respite from the beastly insects when they went to bed, Archie organised two smudge fires on either side of the tents, so that whichever way the wind blew they were certain to be enshrouded in smoke. Morning dawned and Lucy went to fetch the fish — to her horror it had gone, eaten by a mink. Only the backbone remained. All that was left was a tin of baked beans and a tin of tomato soup. This Lucy duly heated up, but the wind got up and bits of grass blew into it. As they were hungry and there was nothing else for breakfast they had to eat what was forever known as 'Lucy's grass soup'.

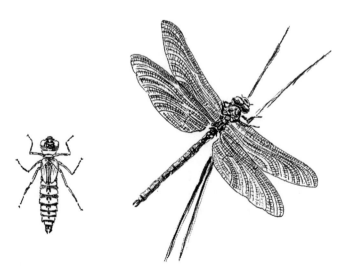

FRESHLY FRIED BROWN TROUT

There are few things quite so delicious as eating an apricot-fleshed trout which you have caught yourself. If you can be bothered to do so, try to fillet it. After the first go it's not so difficult, and you then have more expanse of succulent flesh to embalm in oatmeal and plenty of butter. The system is the same for any fish, even a salmon, though you will need a larger knife for this. If you are on the coast you may decide to go sea fishing and any mackerel you catch are just as good prepared and cooked in the same way.

To fillet a fish:

Step 1. *Cut off head.*

Step 2. *Place fish on board, flat stone, or grassy bank, with tail nearest your tummy and the dorsal fin to the right. Hold body firm with left hand and run knife along backbone.* (If left-handed, read *left* for *right* and vice-versa.)

Step 3. *Ease knife underneath, along rib-cage pulling skin and flesh gently to the left with your left hand until you have uncovered it completely.* ((Read *right* for *left* if left-handed.)

Step 4. *Remove intestines.*

Step 5. *Ease knife under tail end of backbone and lift. You should now be able to pull it off. Your fish will now be lying skin down, opened out in two halves like a book. Remove any major bones.*

To cook:

Fry some rashers of bacon in a little butter and when cooked remove to a plate. Heat plenty of butter until it is foaming and put in the trout, skin side down. Sprinkle flesh with plenty of oatmeal, salt and pepper and cook for a few minutes. Turn over and continue cooking. Repeat procedure with any other fish you intend to eat. Sprinkle more oatmeal in remaining butter and cook for a few seconds until brown. Serve with the bacon, bread and lashings of butter, and strong tea.

Archie maintained that the best tea was as made in the Desert during the war. This involved a billy-can in which the tea-leaves were never thrown away, new ones simply being added to each brew-up, and then ceremonially stewed over a five-gallon drum filled with sand and petrol. At his insistence we did try it once, but it was not a success. I think desert heat, dust, flies and thirst must have been what made it seem, in retrospect, so ambrosial.

SALMON STEAKS IN BUTTER

Should you be camping whilst on a salmon fishing expedition and the gods have smiled on you, there is nothing, absolutely nothing, so exquisite in the gastronomic spectrum as freshly caught salmon. Gut it, cut off thick steaks, melt plenty of butter in your frying pan and cook them for 4 or 5 minutes on each side. Add lemon juice, if you have it, and salt and pepper, and you will realize that it's a different creature altogether from the salmon you buy from the fishmonger's slab. The milky 'curd' between the flakes of fish disappears after a few hours, and it is this which makes it so delectably juicy.

It would be difficult, with only a camp fire or small gas cooker, to emulate Lucy's devotion to *haute cuisine*. She was spending a few days with a friend from university who had taken a vacation job as a ghillie on the Grimester. He was allowed one fish, which he duly caught. He and another friend shared a tumbledown bothy with a very primitive stove. Lucy served the salmon as described above, but with Sauce Hollandaise which she made in a cup over hot water in the kettle.

TRICK OF THE TRADE. To tart up the humble baked beans add a dash of Worcester Sauce, a pinch of mixed herbs and some garlic pepper. Tomato soup will benefit from sugar, garlic pepper and a small slosh of whisky. If you don't believe me, try it and see.

For this kind of camping expedition simplicity is all. Apples and cheese with a hunk of bread will make satisfying 'afters', and don't forget to take plenty of chocolate. You can even melt some in Long Life milk for a bed-time drink, again with a little whisky, and you'll sleep like a log. With all this advice I shall probably be thought to be teaching any grandmothers who read this to suck eggs, but these are just my random and very personal thoughts on the subject.

BARBECUES

This is a wonderful way of cooking, and especially if you have a lot of young to feed as there is nearly always someone who is willing to take charge. If you are in holiday accommodation in Scotland, for example, it might rain for the whole of your stay, so a makeshift kind of barbecue is best. No sense in lugging up a lot of sophisticated, bulky and heavy gear — do-it-yourself is the order of the day.

The best example of this that I can think of was a contraption that I came across in Haringey, North London, where I had gone to deliver some game to a butcher's shop owned by four Greek Cypriot brothers. I had been bidden to the back regions to have my cup of coffee when my nostrils were assailed by a tantalizingly delicious smell of grilled chops. There seemed to be nothing cooking in the kitchen, but when I looked out into the back yard I saw an amazing sight. On an old butcher's block stood a dented aluminium saucepan. Perched on top was a battered colander, which held the burning charcoal, and sizzling away on an iron grid were some pork chops — the Savas brothers' lunch. What made it smell so good was a branch of rosemary, some lemon peel, and a few slices of onion. My own barbecue is a baker's metal tray which has seen better days, with holes punched in the bottom and sides. The metal grill is an oven shelf which came from an obsolete cooker.

Archie was an inveterate mail-order buff, and his best buy was a 'Big Daddy'. What, you may well ask, was (or is) a 'Big Daddy'? It was a five-gallon drum manufactured in three pieces, the bottom one being pierced with holes. You fitted them together and put your grill on top. It was fuelled by newspaper, and eight double pages of the *Telegraph,* each crumpled up to the size of a cricket ball, would cook a pound of sausages perfectly in no time at all. Sadly, our 'Big Daddy' is no more; I wish I could get another one as it was perfect for an impromptu barbecue when the rain stopped and the sun came out.

Fish needs little or no marinading to tenderize it and is best split open (see p.90) and cooked in one of those simple wire gadgets which open out — you stick the fish, steak, chops, or whatever, on one half, fold the other half over and the handles fasten together with a metal ring. In this way the fish does not disintegrate when you turn it over. These gadgets are obtainable from most ironmongers (I got mine from our village shop). All you need to do to the fish is to paint it with olive oil or melted butter, season with salt and pepper, and grill. Experiment with herbs. You may find wild thyme in Scotland or anywhere up in the hills. A branch of juniper laid on the embers is also good.

Believe it or not, you can cook a whole salmon on a barbecue. A friend of mind cooked a 10-lb fish as follows. He painted it with oil and then wrapped it in a whole copy of the *Times*. The entire thing was then dunked in water until it was sodden, then it was laid on the barbecue. It was turned several times and when the newspaper had literally started to char the fish was done — firm, pink and moist. The success of this method was confirmed by another friend, who swears it never fails.

Everyone has their patent marinade. Men, particularly, I notice, seem to come into their own on these occasions, and to hear them swapping recipes for marinades at a barbecue you would think you were listening to a lot of women at a coffee morning. Best-quality meat hardly needs anything to tenderize it, just some olive oil and seasoning, but other cuts such as pork and chicken will benefit as they tend to dry out and can be tasteless.

MARINADES

For any quantity of meat allow 4 fl oz/110 ml per lb/450 g of meat. Cooked marinades flavour the meat more intensely than uncooked ones. They should be allowed to get quite cold before using. Always use a china, glass or enamelled dish in which to immerse the meat, as metal will impart an unpleasant taste. Use a wooden spoon to turn the meat over. Always put your marinating meat in a fridge in a covered container if it is to be soaked for more than 1 hour. The following are basic marinades which will fit in with the simple spices and herbs you will have taken away with you, but add anything which you think will enhance the particular ingredient you are going to barbecue. When you have finished the actual barbecueing you can place a small pan containing any remaining marinade on the embers, reduce it a little and use it as a sauce.

BASIC COOKED MARINADE FOR MEAT

1 stick celery, chopped	1 teaspoon dried thyme
1 carrot, chopped	12 cloves
1 onion, chopped	1 dessertspoon black peppercorns
½ pint/275 ml vinegar	1 dessertspoon redcurrant jelly or demerara
½ pint/275 ml oil	sugar
2 tablespoons parsley, chopped	2 garlic cloves, peeled and crushed
3 bay leaves	

Sauté the vegetables in the oil until golden, then add all the other ingredients and simmer, covered, for 1 hour. Strain and cool. You could use some juniper berries and/or sprigs of rosemary if your holiday is a mixed sporting one and your 'hunter-gatherers' have suddenly returned with a hare or some venison. For half a haunch of venison (unless it is roe, which is smaller) double the marinade quantities and immerse the meat for at least 24 hours, having first cut it into suitable steaks. 12 hours would be sufficient for a saddle of venison or venison loin chops. This marinade keeps in a fridge for 3-4 days.

BEER MARINADE FOR PORK

1½ pints/850 ml beer which has been	1 teaspoon ground ginger
opened and allowed to go flat	3 tablespoons soy sauce
½ pint/275 ml olive or other vegetable oil	½ teaspoon Lea & Perrins Ginger and
1 clove garlic, peeled and crushed	Orange Sauce
½ teaspoon salt	2 tablespoons honey
1 dessertspoon mustard powder	4 tablespoons marmalade

This is particularly delicious and you can also use it for chicken and, at home, for duck breasts (Magret). These can be grilled and allowed to get cold, then sliced thinly and served with a fennel salad.

SIMPLE MARINADE FOR FISH

Trout or salmon will not need any marinade, to my way of thinking, but if you must, here is one which will not distract from the natural flavours.

1 tablespoon lemon juice	*1 teaspoon salt*
4 tablespoons olive oil	*½ teaspoon ground black pepper*

LAURA'S SIMPLE BASIC MARINADE

Laura is a very beautiful American girl. She gave me this very simple recipe, which you can alter to your own taste.

2 tablespoons tomato ketchup	*1 glass dry sherry*
2 tablespoons vegetable oil	*A few drops of tabasco sauce*
2 tablespoons sugar	*1 teaspoon Worcester Sauce*
1 tablespoon wine vinegar	*Salt and pepper*

'Let's have a barbecue!' — in Scotland, at any rate — is a last-minute cry as the sun comes out. It is not something that can be planned in advance (or not in the Highlands, anyway) as tomorrow, or even in a few hours, it might be pouring with rain. So if you do decide to have one, pre-arrange it by marinading your ingredients, if meat, overnight — you can always cook them under the grill or in the oven if it pours with rain at the appointed time. A fish barbecue can be done at the very last minute, since all you need to do is to light the charcoal, let it get really hot, and have to hand oil, salt, pepper and lots of bread and butter. If you've had a bake-up, so much the better, and you can feel really self-sufficient as you eat nutty-tasting, freshly caught trout or sea trout and home-baked soda bread and scones.

NIGHT FISHING
FOR SEA TROUT

Night fishing is not my idea of fun, as I am always terrified of putting my foot in a hole whilst wading, and I find that my fly inevitably gets caught up in a bush. However, sometimes it's the only time when the magical sea trout can be caught.

One of the most weird experiences we had was on a fishing expedition to Wales. We had been given a few days' fishing by a friend, who gave us a map and told us if in trouble to ask at the pub which stood by the bridge where the beats began and ended. We breezed in and asked for information, which was given rather grudgingly, and in a distinctly unfriendly atmosphere. We just put this down to the fact that we came from England and that probably we were going to do the local poachers out of their catch. The truth, however was far more bizarre. . . During the afternoon, as we were fishing, we noticed numbers of people either on foot or on bicycles going up a track on the opposite hillside. What was strange was the fact that each one had a sack over his shoulder which, as seen through our binoculars, seemed to be wriggling. We finally discovered the next day that there had been a cockfight. When the publican found out that we were not police spies he took us into his back parlour and with great pride showed us all the silver spurs which had been won by his father's and grandfather's cocks. He swore that he no longer took part, but I wonder.

You will probably have a high tea before setting out, so a few easily eaten snacks will be best, something that can go into your fishing bag or waistcoat. A thermos of tea or coffee in the car is essential, or even some cocoa to revive the sinking blood-sugar levels.

Choose sandwich fillings which don't fall to bits when you bite into them and which adhere to the bread or roll without dropping into the river. Anything like tomato or lettuce is hopeless unless mixed thoroughly with a good binding mixture. If using slices of bread, cut off the crusts and when you have made the sandwiches press well together and cut into 4 or 6. Bridge rolls fatly filled are a good idea, and if you have to use baps hollow out as much of the inside as possible, put in lots of filling, and cut in four. The object of all this is to have food which can be eaten in one or two mouthfuls, thereby not endangering the smooth casting of the fisherman as he endeavours to cover every inch of the water in the dark. A good, rich, moist fruit cake cut into bite-sized pieces and some bars of chocolate will stave off the pangs of hunger until breakfast.

IDEAS FOR SNACKS AND SANDWICHES

1. Samosas, cocktail-sized sausage rolls.

2. Ham, coarsely ground and mixed with butter, mustard and a suspicion of marmalade.

3. Mini-pitta bread filled with mince flavoured with curry powder and chutney and mixed with cream cheese.

4. Bridge rolls filled with cooked salmon mixed with mayonnaise and dill weed.

5. Bap filled with coarsely ground chicken (one or two sharp bursts in the Magimix), with chopped hard-boiled egg and chopped parsely, bound together with a little white sauce, well seasoned with salt and pepper.

6. Sandwich or roll filled with Cheddar or other hard cheese processed with spring onion, Branston Pickle and butter.

7. Scotch pancakes or scones spread with butter beaten with a little jam or honey, cut into flour.

NANNY'S SCOTTISH GINGERBREAD

This is a really dark, heavy gingerbread — good ballast for the hungry fisherman.

8 oz/225 g butter	2 eggs, well beaten
8 oz/225 g muscovado sugar (any soft brown sugar will do as substitute)	2 tablespoons dried ground ginger
	1 tablespoon powdered cinnamon
8 oz/225 g black treacle	1 teaspoon bicarbonate of soda
8 oz/225 g plain flour	¼ pint/275 ml hot milk

Cream butter and sugar in Magimix or by hand. Add the treacle, eggs and spices. Dissolve the bicarbonate of soda in the hot milk and beat into the mixture, sprinkle in the flour, mix well, then spoon into a well-greased tin. Bake in a pre-heated oven at 325°F/150°C/Gas Mark 2 for 2½ hours. Turn out when cold.

FRUIT CAKE

This will keep well so you can make it at home whenever convenient and take it away with you.

8 oz/225 g self-raising flour	5 oz/150 g butter
1 teaspoon mixed spice	5 oz/150 g sugar (I use demerara or light soft brown sugar)
1 teaspoon bicarbonate of soda	
½ teaspoon salt	1 tablespoon golden syrup
2 oz/50 g candied peel, chopped	¼ pint/150 ml milk
12 oz/250 g mixed dried fruit	1 good tablespoon brandy, rum or dark sweet sherry
2 oz/50 g glacé cherries, halved and rolled in flour	

Cream butter, sugar and syrup in the Magimix, or by hand until light and fluffy. Sieve the flour, soda, salt and spices and add to the creamed butter mixture alternately with the milk. Mix the peel and fruit together and add last. Scrape into a basin, cover with cling-film and leave overnight. The following day add the liquor of your choice and stir well. Grease an 8-inch/20-cm cake tin and flour lightly, then line with well-buttered greaseproof paper and turn mixture into the tin. Pre-heat oven to 350°F/175°C/Gas Mark 4 and place the tin on centre shelf. Cook for 2 hours then turn heat down to 325°F/160°C/Gas Mark 3 for a further 30 minutes. Cool slightly and turn out onto a rack. When quite cold wrap in foil and put in a tin. Keep for a few days before eating.

I hope you will have found some new ideas from this book. I have tried to get away from stereotyped menus and recipes, but have also included some really old-fashioned British dishes to slot into what I thought were appropriate scenarios. You can always pick something from one section and use it in any other context, even a dinner party at home. As always my cry is 'use your loaf'; if you haven't got an ingredient or seasoning specified in a recipe, try something else — you may have made the discovery of the year. Imagination usually pays.

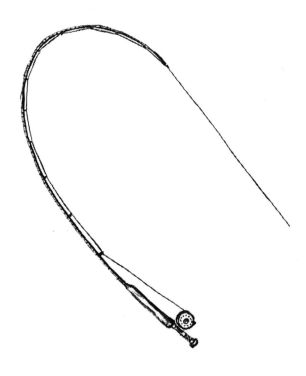

INDEX

Entries in **bold** type denote recipes and the page numbers for them.